A Handy-Dandy Guide to Mumbo-Jumbo, Jibber-Jabber,
And other
Reduplicated Words and Phrases

By

"Lazlo Maslow"

A Handy-Dandy Guide to Mumbo-Jumbo, Jibber-Jabber, and other Reduplicated Words and Phrases

ISBN 978-1-71690-883-5 Imprint: Lulu.com

Trademarks

All terms that are known to be trademarks or service marks have been appropriately identified as such on each usage. The author cannot attest to the accuracy of this information. Use of a term in this book should not be regarded as affecting the validity of any trademark or service mark.

Warning and Disclaimer

Every effort has been made to make this book as complete and accurate as possible, but no warranty or fitness is implied. This information is provided on an "as is" basis. The author and the publisher shall have neither liability nor responsibility to any person or entity with respect to loss or damages arising from the information or from the use of the information contained in this book.

Copyright and Usage Questions

Questions relating to copyright matters or regarding usage of this book should be directed to the copyright owner via email:
kelvin@westallmurray.com

Introduction

In anticipation of the likelihood that very few people will read this introduction, I will be relatively brief.

What a delightful linguistic phenomenon reduplication is! In the English language, reduplication often adds a folksy, lighthearted slant to what is being said or written. Saying that you overheard two friends having a vicious, fierce argument is rather harsh and direct, but saying that they were, "Having a right old _ding-dong_" softens the description of the incident, leaving the details to the imagination of your listener.

Of course, many reduplicated expressions are somewhat scathing. Others are euphemisms for potentially unappetizing topics.

So what exactly is reduplication? Well, the best way to understand the concept is to look at a few examples in this book. In terms of a _formal_ definition, one might say that reduplication is a morphological linguistic process whereby an entire word, or even just a part of a word, is repeated either exactly or with a small modification.

As mentioned, the English language makes extensive and creative use of reduplication to add interest and variety to the written and spoken word. Some other languages employ the concept as a formal component of their grammar. For example, in Malayo-Polynesian languages reduplication can be used to form plurals. In Indonesian, _pulau_ means island, and _pulau-pulau_ means islands.

Well, enough of the technicalities. I risk descending into _geek-speak_ at this rate. Before you dive in to the terms and expressions in the book, though, I have just a couple of comments for you.

Despite the 260-plus entries below, this little book just scratches the surface of the remarkable number of reduplicated phrases that exist. I could have continued for years documenting additional examples, but had to draw a line somewhere. Indeed, the emergence and use of these terms seem to be proliferating. The ever-developing realm of social media, coupled with the constant appearance of new businesses and commercial models, means that new, catchy terms, and names for companies and products, are always being sought. Accordingly, many current occurrences of reduplication form the name, of or part of the name of, business products or entities. As a general rule I have tried to select just a few such corporate examples for inclusion, focusing more on historical or current everyday spoken or written uses of reduplication.

The format I have used in the book is to arrange the entries alphabetically, so the need for a table of contents or index is redundant. Feel free to browse, dabble, or read sequentially as you see fit.

Many friends and family members have helped me put this book together, either by simple encouragement or by offering suggested terms for inclusion. To all of those individuals, I acknowledge my sincerely-held debt of deep gratitude.

Okey-dokey, enough of this introductory *clap-trap* I hear you muttering. Let's get to the *nitty-gritty*!

Kelvin Murray (Lazlo Maslow), Virginia, USA, 2020.

AIRY-FAIRY

This is a suitably ethereal term to start us off on our journey.
Some, indeed, might say that only airy-fairy types would even
open a book like this, let alone spend any time enjoying its
contents.

So, *airy fairy* then. Used correctly as an adjective, airy-fairy
conjures up images of either people or ideas that lack true
connection to the real world of work, paying bills, fixing
broken door locks, and all the other mundane aspects of life.
"Here we are, trying to pull this truck out of the ditch, and the
boss keeps giving us airy-fairy advice about fulcrums, levers
and moments! Why can't he just shut up and lend a hand?"

Airy-fairy ideas are not grounded in reality. Like the sprites to
which the expression alludes, airy-fairy people seem to drift
through life without regard to the irritation and burden they
place on other people.

ALLY-PALLY

"Let's go down the <u>*rub-a-dub*</u>, then head up to *Ally Pally* for
the motorcycle show!"

Ally Pally is an affectionate contraction of the name Alexandra
Palace, an entertainment and sports venue located in the
London Borough of Haringey. Opened in 1873, Alexandra
Palace has had a complex history of ownership and usage over
the years. Major fires destroyed much the structure, first in
1873 shortly after the grand opening, and then once again in
1980. The BBC started television broadcasts from Alexandra
Palace in 1936, and broadcasts continued from there until
1956. During the Second World War, the transmitting
antennae were re-roled to perform jamming of the navigation
systems of German bomber aircraft. At the time of writing,
Alexandra Palace is operated by the Alexandra Park and
Palace Charitable Trust, a registered charity.

ARTSY-FARTSY

Like many of the adjectives in this book, *Artsy-Fartsy* can apply to people, to their thoughts, ideas and behavior, to products and artifacts, and even to general characteristics of pretty much anything that has a noun or abstract noun as its name! "I went to the coffee shop yesterday for a quiet coffee. The place was full of artsy-fartsy _beardie-weirdies_ reciting poetry! It's called a poetry slam, they have them every Tuesday."

Artsy-fartsy means that something is overly decorative or elaborate, and probably impractical, for its intended purpose. People too can exhibit artsy-fartsy characteristics and behavior. If so, their ideas are probably _airy-fairy_ in equal measure.

The term's derivation, of course, stems from art and fart.

ANDY PANDY

One of my fond childhood memories is of watching the television show, *Watch with Mother*, with my mother, on our black and white flickering television set. The show was broadcast at lunchtimes on the only channel available at the time, the BBC. We used to watch it every weekday until, at the age of five, I started primary school. In addition to being mildly educational for children, the show provided wonderful entertainment. Some of the embedded mini-stories included, "Bill and Ben (The Flower Pot Men)", "The Wooden Tops", "Muffin the Mule" and, *Andy Pandy*".

Andy Pandy was a puppet or marionette. He lived in a picnic basket. He had two friends: one was a teddy bear called (of course) Teddy, and another was a rag doll called Looby Loo. She, Looby Loo had her own special song, "Here we go Looby Loo". (Needless to say that song is now stuck in my head as I type this entry!) At the end of each episode, all three would go back to the picnic basket, and would sing, "Time to go home, Time to go home, Andy is waving goodbye."

The inspiration for the Andy Pandy character may have been Paul Atterbury, who was the young son of Audrey Atterbury, one of the puppeteers.

ANGUISH LANGUISH

In 1956, Prentice-Hall published a book by Howard L. Chace titled *Anguish Languish*. The work contained poems and stories, many of them well-known, but written in a made-up language called Anguish Languish. This was not really a language at all, but rather a homophonic translation. As an example, the tale of Little Red Riding Hood was titled, "Ladle Rat Rotten Hut" with real English near-homophonic words substituted for the originals. As a further example, within the same story the phrase "A nervous sausage bag ice!" was used instead of "I never saw such big eyes!"

If you are wondering why on earth anyone would undertake such an exercise, then Howard Chace's own explanation might (or might not) shed some light: "The Anguish Languish consists only of the purest of English words, and its chief raison d'être is to demonstrate the marvelous versatility of a language in which almost anything can, if necessary, be made to mean something else."

As a somewhat related matter, those of you who have ever travelled along Interstate 95 in the USA, especially on the stretch between Georgia and North Carolina, may have noticed the many billboard signs for the retail outlet/attraction known as South of the Border. The border in question is the North Carolina/South Carolina border, but the establishment nevertheless presents an overall Mexican theme. Many of the billboards involve puns that reflect English and/or Spanish colloquial expressions. The one that comes to mind as I write this entry about Anguish Languish reads, "You never sausage a place!" and has a picture of a giant sausage to attract the eye of the traveler.

Tangentially-related to Anguish Languish, the book, *Mots D'Heures: Gousses, Rames: The D'Antin Manuscript (Mother Goose's Rhymes)*, was published in 1967 by Luis d'Antin van Rooten. As the name suggests, the book transcribes common nursery rhymes/Mother Goose rhymes into similar sounding but nonsensical French sentences. The opening line from Humpty Dumpty for example, *Humpty Dumpty sat on a wall*, appears as, "Un petit d'un petit s'étonne aux halles". Great fun!

AYE-AYE

I almost forgot to include this term, but remembered to do so while thinking about what I should write concerning *Tit-for-Tat* later in this book. Why? Well, I was thinking that, "An eye for an eye" is a good example of *tit-for-tat* behavior, and, "Aye-aye, Captain!" sprung into my mind. Such is the pervasive power of reduplicated phrases!

Back to aye-aye, the component "aye" is a way of indicating assent or agreement, sometimes in a formal setting. The Speaker of the British Parliamentary House of Commons, and other officials in similar roles, may announce the result of a vote by including the phrase, "The ayes have it". In this sense, aye equates directly to yea.

Dialectically, aye usually means yes. In Scots, aye is a more common word for indicating the affirmative than is yes. In nautical parlance, *aye-aye* is the correct way to acknowledge a command or order from someone of higher rank. It means that the order is understood and that it will be complied with promptly.

An animal called the aye-aye, Daubentonia madagascariensis, is a species of long-fingered lemur native to Madagascar.

ARGY-BARGY

This term conjures up images of argumentative people
pushing and shoving and behaving in a generally oafish
manner. "Hey, calm down everyone and wait in line, quietly.
Argy-bargy won't get you served any quicker." Such people
can display their lack of social sensitivity in traffic, on aircraft,
in lines or queues for service, or simply in everyday encounters
with the rest of us reasonable people.

The author noticed an upsurge in the use of this phrase in
Britain about the time of the 1982 Falkland Islands Conflict: a
brief war between Britain and Argentina regarding the
sovereignty of the Falkland Islands, a British possession in the
South Atlantic. The Argentinian view was that the Falklands,
known to them as the Malvinas, were Argentine territory. To
divert attention from its own unpopularity, in 1982 the ruling
Argentinian Military Junta decided to invade the islands,
aiming to create a jingoistic sense of national pride. In this
aim it was successful, but with the invasion and capture it was
unsuccessful. A task force of Navy, Air Force and Army
personnel and assets was dispatched from Britain, and it
liberated the islands. In the popular British press the
Argentinians had become simply, "the Argies". And because
the invasion itself had been considered rather un-British,
pushy behavior, "Argy-Bargy" seemed an appropriate way to
label the aggression.

For a tangentially-related topic, please refer to *Ding-Dong*
later in this volume.

BEANIE-WEENIE

This makes me hungry just thinking about the term. In the
United States, *beanie-weenie* is a "comfort food", much as
beans-on-toast is in the United Kingdom. You can make your
own beanie-weenie, and also buy variants in cans readymade.
Van Camp, for example, sells cans of this delightful dish under

the trademarked name, "Beanee Weenee"®. In addition to its
wonderful culinary attributes, the meal is also inexpensive.
"We had some unexpected bills this month, so it's beanie-
weenie suppers for the whole family for a while."

Basically the food is baked beans (navy beans) in sauce with
hot dog chunks mixed in. In the canned versions, the hot dogs
are sometimes mini dogs rather than chunks of full size dogs.
So how come, "Weenie"? Well, the frankfurters served in hot
dogs are often known as "wieners". (Incidentally, other
sausage-shaped items are sometimes referred to as wieners as
well!) The name is derived from the German word for Vienna,
i.e. Wien. So "wiener" refers to something or someone from
Vienna. Needless to say, not all hot dogs come from Vienna,
but some sausages do.

As a sideline, another "comfort food" is small cans of "Vienna
Sausages", sometimes pronounced "Vie'-ee-nah". These cans
fit nicely in a handbag ("purse" or "pocket-book") with some
crackers. Tasty!

BEARDIE-WEIRDY

"Waste of time going to have a drink at the King's Arms
tonight. It's a folk music evening. The place will be full of
beardie-weirdies telling you to be quiet if you dare to talk
during any of that nasal singing that they like so much."

Use of this expression was at its height around the year 2014.
At that time, beards were less common than a few years later.
Indeed, at the time there was an apparent high concentration
of beards amongst any gathering of individuals with an overly-
developed fascination for a particular hobby or activity.
Usually the hobby in question will be one where most non-
adherents would consider it to be a very boring or odd
pastime. Beardie-weirdy types tended to gravitate towards
one another.

Note: simply having a beard does not automatically make one
a beardie-weirdy. Likewise, someone can have the
characteristics of a beardie-weirdy even if he (or she) is clean-
shaven.

Note 2: beards come and go in fashion!

BEAVER FEVER

This refers to an affliction suffered by some lonely long-
distance truckers in the USA, whereby the affected individual
has a near-uncontrollable longing for intimacy with a female
partner.

BEE'S KNEES

"I had never cared much for pumpkin pie, but the slice your
aunt served me was the *bee's knees*!"

This rather odd phrase, indicating that something exhibits
excellence or high quality, is of uncertain origin. Some believe
the usage to be derived from Bee Jackson, a famous dancer of
the Charleston in the 1920s. Others think it is a modification
of "business", as in, "That pie was the business!" Another
theory is that the term is a deliberate reversal of its meaning in
early Victorian times, when saying that something was as weak
as, or as small as, a bee's knees, was a more common saying.
As with many of the phrases in this book, more vulgar
equivalents have arisen. "That's the dog's bollocks", for
example, is a way of saying that something stands out, much
as a dog's bollocks literally do.

BIGWIG

Not strictly a reduplicated word nowadays, but originally so,
bigwig is now quite common as a single word. An example of
usage might be, "Let's go for a meal in that restaurant on

Pennsylvania Avenue, and rub shoulders with some of the bigwigs from Capitol Hill!"

The term originated from that strange period of European sartorial history when people of standing started to wear ever more elaborate and grandiose wigs as part of their daily attire. Starting around 1655 it became common for people to shave their natural hair as a preventative for head lice. Sometimes the shaving was also necessary because a person's own hair was becoming patchy or disfigured as a result of venereal disease. The fad was triggered by Louis XIV of France (to cover his thinning hair), and by his cousin Charles II of England (to hide his grey hair). Immediately, courtesans followed suit. The wigs that were worn were often doused with scented powder to help cover the rancid smell that they might otherwise acquire. Wigs, and powder, were expensive. Before long, the size of a wig became a direct indicator of the wealth of the wearer.

The wig-wearing craze had run its course by the end of the 18th century. The French Revolution led to the abandonment of wigs, as too did the levying of a tax on wig powder in Britain in 1795. Personally, I believe that an additional factor was the ridicule heaped upon British establishment figures and redcoat officers leading up to and after American independence. American patriots viewed wigs as signs of effeminacy, especially in light of the fact that the British were scornful of the colonists for *not* wearing wigs. Indeed, the wording of the song, Yankee Doodle was originally written by the British to be condescending to the locals. "He put a feather in his cap and called it macaroni", suggests that the poor common American could only adorn himself with a feather, rather than with a grand wig. ("Macaroni" in the song refers to the Macaroni Club, a drinking club for "dandies" in London in the 1770s. Members of that club would have been more than able to purchase a wig.)

BIZZY LIZZY

"*Bizzy Lizzy®*" was the name of a child's doll produced by the
Ideal Novelty and Toy Company from 1971 to 1972. The key
characteristic of the doll was that it was sold with an ironing
board, iron, feather duster, manual carpet sweeper, and a
battery pack to power the doll as it performed various
household chores. Even when first introduced, the doll was
mildly controversial in some quarters due to perceived
behavioral and role stereotyping.

BUSY LIZZIE

In the United Kingdom, *Busy Lizzie* is the common name for
the house plant Impatiens walleriana. The plant is native to
eastern Africa, from Kenya to Mozambique. The Latin species
name walleriana was chosen in honor of British missionary
Horace Waller.

BLAME GAME

"You have to be joking! Go to the Project Lessons-Learned
session? It'll just be one big *blame game!*"

A "Lessons-Learned Exercise" is an event often scheduled by
organizations towards the end of, or after completion of, a
major project or organizational initiative. Although such
exercises are intended to identify what went well in addition to
what did not go so well, many attendees resort to focusing on
the negative lessons, and pointing fingers at the perceived
guilty parties. As a result, the term "blame game" does tend to
be a more accurate description of the proceedings. The
tendency to refer to Lessons Learned exercises as "Project
Post-mortems", or "Project Autopsies", does nothing to
improve the way in which such events are conducted!

BLING-BLING

Bling-bling, sometimes simply bling, refers to ostentatious jewelry of often questionable taste. The words are onomatopoeic in nature, highlighting the clinking of the items being so described. In addition to jewelry, the term can be used for any accessories that are worn or carried, and even to cosmetic medical enhancements such as gold or diamond-studded tooth caps. The term originates from hip hop culture, becoming popular after it was featured in the 1999 song, "Bling Bling" by Cash Money Millionaires.

BLING RING

The Bling Ring is a movie that was released in June 2013. The plot has to do with a group of fame-obsessed teenagers who track the whereabouts of celebrities so that they can then rob the celebrities' homes when the celebrities are not in residence. The irony is that while the film was being premiered at the Cannes film festival in May 2013, a real robbery took place at the Novotel Hotel in Cannes. Over $1 million worth of Chopard jewelry was stolen from a hotel-room safe. One of the Swiss jeweler's employees was staying in the room. The gems were intended for loaning out to celebrities for red-carpet events. Everyone involved in the *Bling Ring* movie quickly disavowed any knowledge of the theft (while possibly welcoming the associated fall-out publicity).

BLUE'S CLUES

Although many, many television show names have used reduplicative titles over the years, I am including *Blue's Clues* for a particular reason. *Blue's Clues* was an American educational children's television series that ran on Nickelodeon for 10 years from 1996. The show featured live action as well as animation. The plot revolved around a blue-spotted dog named Blue who would leave a trail of clues and paw prints for the host and the viewers to deduce her plans for the day. A successor series, *Blue's Clues & You!* premiered on November 11, 2019.

So why have I included *Blue's Clues*? Well, one of the artifacts used by the show's host while decoding various clues was the "*Handy Dandy* Notebook and Pen". This same item, in the UK version of the show, was called the "*Super Duper* Notebook". Perhaps while watching *Blue's Clues* with our then young son *Nater-Tater*, the pervasive influence of reduplication really embedded itself in my mind as a topic of linguistic fascination.

BODGE-JOB

"What do you call that?" someone might ask. "Your job was to help me caulk these windows, not smear the stuff all over the side of the house. Look, it's not even straight, and look at those lumps! What a *bodge-job*!"

To bodge something is a long-standing term for doing a shoddy, *slap-dash* piece of work. So a bodge-job is simply the result of bodging something. Sometimes, *botch* is used as an alternate to bodge. Shakespeare used the term, "bodged" in his play *Henry VI* (Part 3, Act 1, Scene 4).

Oddly, the term bodging can also be used for one very specific, highly-skilled, trade, namely the turning of chair legs from recently-harvested, unseasoned hardwood. Chair bodgers would travel from location to location in southern England, turning chair legs on-site at a woodland location. Often, a bodger would use a traditional "pole lathe" to turn the wood, made right at the work site consisting of a springy sapling and foot lever to impart a spinning motion to the wood blanks.

BOOGIE WOOGIE

A music genre with its heyday in the 1920s, but originating in African-American communities in the 1870s. The genre is a form of fast blues piano. The term can also refer to the form of swing dance for which the music is the accompaniment. *Boogie woogie* greatly influenced big band, country and gospel music. The single word, "Boogie" in its own right has acquired multiple meanings relating to dancing, moving quickly, leaving a location, and many more.

For me personally, I exercise great caution when pronouncing the words boogie woogie. If I accidentally pronounce the double O's to rhyme with "fool" rather than with "look", my wife is likely to kick my behind!

BOOB-TUBE

A *boob-tube* is an article of adult female attire that takes the form or a tight, sleeveless cylinder of stretchy material that extends from around the navel upwards to underarm level, leaving the shoulders bare. The compression of the fabric renders additional support in the form of a brassiere unnecessary, but the sartorial elegance of the outfit can be enhanced if brassier straps are visible above the top of the boob-tube. In British English, the term Tube Top is often used as a slightly more polite, but less descriptive way of describing this delightful garment.

An additional, perhaps dated, meaning of boob-tube in the United States was as a condescending slang term for television. The equivalent term goggle-box in the United Kingdom was used in a similarly disparaging way. In both cases, these terms alluded to the apparent mindlessness of vast swathes of the viewership while they absorbed whatever was being served up to them for information (or mis-information) and entertainment.

BOOT-SCOOT

This is an alternate term for the country music dance form
better known as a line dance. I have also heard the term used
to refer to a country music dance event. Tying both this and
the previous dance-related entry, above, is a song called, "Boot
Scootin' Boogie", recorded by the band Asleep at the Wheel for
their album, *Keepin' Me Up Nights* released in 1990. The song
was later covered by various performers, including the country
music duo Brooks & Dunn.

BOW-WOW

The sound of a barking dog? Well, maybe. Dogs' barks can be
onomatopoeically rendered in various ways in the English
language. Both *bow-wow* and *woof-woof* tend to imply a
rather friendly barking, at least to my ear. It is interesting to
me also, that languages other than English often denote
animal sounds differently.   For example, dogs don't "say"
woof in Cantonese, Romanian, Spanish, Japanese or
Indonesian. Instead, the respective terms in these languages
are, *Wong, Ham, Guau, Wan* and *Guk*.

BRAIN DRAIN

"We keep losing our best employees. As soon as they get some
experience they head off to America.....bloody *Brain Drain*!"

This term was much more prevalent in the 1960s than it is
today, at least in Britain where the usage originated. Back
then, not long after World War II, Britain's influence in the
world was waning. At the same time the US was continuing its
ascendance in industrial and scientific preeminence. The
result was that the most skilled scientists and engineers were
in greater demand outside of Britain than within it. After
graduating from leading universities and after some time in
the workplace, experts and leading thinkers in various fields
were finding well paid positions in the US, and were

emigrating. This loss of expertise at the cutting edge further exacerbated the declining global influence of the UK. The "brain drain" was a favorite topic in newspaper editorials, bemoaning the woes and troubles of then modern day Britain.

In the late twentieth century everything began to change. The US still needed more skilled scientists and engineers than it could produce internally, but now the sources of the missing skills shifted to India and later China, and also to Eastern European and West Asian countries. In such areas there were huge pools of exceptional talent, but in many cases the local salaries were considerably lower than those in the US or even the UK. Various Visa schemes were put in place to make it easier to import talent (such as the H1b visa). At the same time, a growing backlash from US Nationals raised the issue of the need to preserve employment prospects for natural-born US citizens. Essentially, in the twenty-first century the mobility of specialized expertise and labor across national boundaries has rendered the term "brain drain" somewhat anachronistic.

BRIC-A-BRAC

"Before we pack for the move to the new house I want to drastically root out some of our *bric-a-brac*."

Accumulated personal detritus and debris that the owner simply cannot bring himself or herself to consign to the waste receptacle, can be described as bric-a-brac. In most kitchens, at least one drawer will be stuffed with such material. Batteries that may or may not have remaining life, unidentifiable spare keys, maybe a chocolate or two, are examples. The term applies equally to larger items such as ornaments, furniture, broken radio-controlled toys, paper and electronic documents from jobs held many decades earlier, and other sundries. Many items of bric-a-brac power the very lucrative self-storage industry.

BREW THRU

Brew Thru is the name of a business, with many close imitators, located on the Outer Banks of North Carolina, a vacation destination. Here, one may purchase beer by the crate and have it loaded into one's car or truck, all without having to exit the vehicle. Wonderful!

BUMPER HUMPER

"My car is getting repaired. A *bumper-humper* rear-ended me on the way to work yesterday."

Yes, this term is permeated with sexual allusion. It refers to a habitual tailgater, a driver who travels far too close to the car in front. Close enough, indeed, to mean that there is no way that the offender can avoid striking the car being followed if the lead car slows suddenly. The term conjures up images of unwanted amorous attention, and rightly so. Tailgaters are basically morons. The US Highway Transportation Safety Agency recently upgraded its advice on "following distances" from a recommended 2 seconds worth of interval between cars to 3 seconds. The problem with the guidance, good as it is, is that most people have no idea how long a second is! I have actually challenged people when I am a passenger and said, "Aren't you supposed to be 2 seconds behind that car?" The reply was usually, "I am 2 seconds behind, one-two, see! Anyway, it's the same thing as 2 car lengths!" What? Two car lengths? At 60 miles per hour, a car travels 176 feet in two seconds, not 2 car lengths. If you think I am obsessed with this, you are correct. I have spent countless hours in stopped traffic, all because of rear-end crashes caused by moronic bumper-humping tailgaters.

CACKY-LACKY

Cacky-Lacky is an affectionate term used by some residents of the Carolinas in the USA to refer to the State of North

Carolina. As mentioned later in this volume, the equivalent appellation for South Carolina is _Sacky-Lacky_.

CHALK TALK

This refers to a type of briefing or lecture where the speaker illustrates various points and topics in real time, drawing with chalk on a blackboard, or more recently using markers and a dry-erase board. Such talks differ from briefings using pre-prepared graphics or presentation slides, in that they are created and delivered live. Delivery of *chalk talks* became a performance art in the late nineteenth and early twentieth centuries, with some artists achieving fame or notoriety, appearing in vaudeville shows and other public venues. Chalk talks were also common at religious rallies.

One specific use of the term is associated with the sport of hashing (see _hash-bash_ and _hash-cash_). A chalk talk is the briefing to participants ahead of a hash, explaining the routes and methods of marking of the trails (often marked by chalk).

CHARLEY FARLEY

Between 1971 and 1982, one of the best-loved television shows in Britain was *The Two Ronnies*, a comedy sketch show devised by Bill Cotton for the BBC. The stars of the show were Ronnie Barker and Ronnie Corbett. Amongst many one-off sketches, the show usually included an ongoing comedy drama serial story which continued through the eight episodes in a series. Four of these serials were spoof detective mysteries, featuring the investigators "Piggy Malone" (Ronnie Barker) and "Charley Farley" (Ronnie Corbett). Charley Farley was always introduced as, "Charley Farley, BA", and he appeared wearing a traditional British university-style neck scarf. To this day, whenever I see someone's name written with the suffix "BA" appended, I always hear in my mind the expression, "Charley Farley, BA"!

CHICK FLICK

A *chick flick* is a film/movie that most would deem as appealing more to a female audience than to a male audience. Stereotypes aside, this term typically implies that a particular movie is likely to generate the type of emotions that may necessitate the use of a handkerchief or tissue to soak up tears. Man movies, on the other hand, are likely to stimulate cries of, "Yeah, kick his ass!" during intense scenes of action or retribution.

CHIN-CHIN

The phrase *chin-chin* is a rather dated equivalent to "Cheers", and is said by some people before partaking of a beverage in a social gathering. Chin-chin is more commonly heard in British English than in other variants of the English language, and most probably is of empire or colonial origin. Various proposed etymologies exist. The most plausible is that the term derives from pidgin Chinese, where *tsing-tsing* was sometimes used to mean "please" or "please take". *Cin cin* is also used in Italian as a pre-drink salutation, pronounced in the same way as the English chin-chin.

In Japanese, *chinchin* is a slang term for penis. This means that one might wish to avoid the phrase chin-chin as a way of toasting a group of Japanese business people. Likewise, the words that the Three Little Pigs say to the wolf, "Not by the hairs of my chinny-chin-chin", might cause a degree of baffled consternation when quoted to a Japanese audience.

CHIT-CHAT

The sort of idle, insincere verbal interaction that is both pointless and annoying in equal measure may be referred to as *chit-chat*. Often, chit-chat provides a filler during otherwise awkward silences. Many people do, of course, feel uncomfortable when little is being said.

There are some emerging cultural norms that may be increasing the amount of chit-chat experienced by us all. The broadcast industry, radio in particular, espouses the need to avoid "dead air" at all costs. Nature abhors a vacuum, and radio producers abhor absence of sound. As a result, presenters feel compelled to fill natural silences with something audible to the listeners, including vacuous prattle. Needless to say, life imitates art, and so more and more people are starting to speak faster in their daily lives and personal interactions, leaving shorter gaps between sentences and paragraphs, and moving from thought to thought and from concept to concept in their verbal deliveries at a faster rate. "Say something, anything" seems to by a mantra guiding behavior. Quantity of content, and its delivery velocity, have become less important than quality of information. Many streamers and on-line personalities edit their presentations after recording to remove inter-sentence pauses, where they would naturally inhale or exhale. The resulting finished product is often a cacophonous onslaught of sound delivered at a literally breathless pace.

CHOCK-A-BLOCK

When something (a container, a room, a location, or anything that "holds" other items) is full to capacity, and those items are crammed together, its condition might be referred to as *chock-a-block*. A similar term is chock-full, but the expressions have different origins. Chock-a-block probably derives from nautical usage. A block is a component of a block-and-tackle device that uses pulleys and ropes to haul heavy items vertically on a ship, possibly to load cargo or to raise components of rigging (spars, booms) up to the sails. The block component contains one or more pulleys, and often more than one block is used to increase lifting power. If the ropes are pulled completely tight, the blocks might be pulled tight together, and the system could become chock-a-block. Chock-full on the other hand seems to go back to the Middle English term *chokkefull*, meaning full to choking point.

CHOO-CHOO

This book would be seriously deficient if *choo-choo* were not included. Almost certainly, choo-choo was the first reduplicated expression I heard as a baby, and quite possibly the words choo-choo were some of the first words of any type I ever heard.

A choo-choo, of course, is a train, or more specifically a steam locomotive. Choo-choos formed part of my earliest nurturing experiences. When I was very young, my father worked for British Railways. In addition, at least once a week I would walk with my mother to the local station, a whistle-stop "halt", where passengers had to flag down any train they wanted to board. We would then travel to the nearby market town to buy groceries, and return by train through the beautiful Devon countryside.

Sadly, to many people, the words choo-choo would be frowned upon as "baby talk" that no enlightened parent would use in front of their child for risk of damaging the child's linguistic abilities. Piffle! My own linguistic skills are at least average, although some might say that I would not be writing this book if my parents' use of the term choo-choo had not scrambled my thinking at a young age.

Choo-choo is potentially a somewhat confusing term to current generations of children. I have yet to hear a diesel or electric locomotive emit any sound remotely resembling "choo-choo". The term remains in widespread use, nevertheless. Many children's songs are associated with choo-choos, and many restaurants and other businesses include the words.

CHOW-CHOW

Chow-chow is a pickled relish common in some areas of North America. The exact recipe varies regionally, either consisting mainly of cabbage, or containing a broader range of ingredients such as tomatoes, onions, carrots, beans, asparagus, cauliflower and peas. After pickling and canning, chow-chow is used as a condiment. It is similar in style to the relish known in England as piccalilli.

The origin of the name "chow-chow" is debated. Some hold that the relish arrived in the Southern United States with the Acadian (Cajun) people after they were expelled from Nova Scotia, with the name being derived from the French word for cabbage, *chou*. Others believe the name may be of Chinese or (Asian) Indian origin. It is certainly the case that *chow chow* is used in Nepal and in some other Asian countries as a term for dried instant noodles.

Chow when used as a single word is a slang term for food, and to chow down means to consume food enthusiastically. US armed forces personnel visit the chow-hall (canteen or mess hall) to chow-down. The term tuck-in in the United Kingdom is used in a similar way to chow-down. Someone who enjoys food to a greater than average extent might be referred to as a chowhound.

Operation Chowhound and the preceding Operation Manna were humanitarian food drops, carried out to relieve a famine in the German-occupied Netherlands, undertaken by Allied bomber crews during the final days of World War II in Europe.

In a non-food context, a chow chow, or chow, is a breed of domestic dog that originated from China. Its Chinese name is *Songshi-Quan*, meaning puffy-lion dog.

CHROME-DOME

Chrome dome is a disparaging term for a (usually male) person who suffers from loss of hair on the head. "Folically challenged" is a tongue in cheek term meaning the same thing, and one which is often used by persons so afflicted themselves.

Overall I would say that the term chrome-dome is archaic these days, which is good in many ways. Being condescending about someone's appearance is a terrible way to behave. Additionally, the common practice whereby men just shave their heads once hair loss starts to develop, means that bald heads have become far more commonplace.

CLAP-TRAP

This refers to nonsensical talk, often delivered in a pompous way to incur approval or admiration from one's audience. Personally I prefer "piffle" as a near synonym to this term, mainly because I always picture a monocle-wearing old curmudgeon bellowing, "Piffle!" if someone is talking *clap-trap*. The origin of clap-trap, or claptrap, seems to be from a device of that name used in theaters from around 1730 or so to incite applause from an audience. Such a device would be employed much as laughter tracks are added to sit-coms to convince a remote audience that a show is actually funny. In theatrical use, claptrap came to be used to refer to any type of technique or gag that could be used to solicit applause.

CLIP-CLOP

This is a straightforward onomatopoeic term to describe the sound of horses' hooves beating on a hard surface. Generally it would be used in relation to slow-moving horses, such as draught horses. "I heard the rag-and-bone man's horse *clip-clop*ping down the street through my open window, along with the creaking and clanking of his iron cart wheels on the cobblestones."

COUNTY MOUNTY

County Mounty is a trucker/CB radio term used in the USA to refer to a member of a local-jurisdiction police force, or possibly to his or her police car. County Mounties are distinct from State police or highway patrol staff.

COCK-BLOCK

I have heard this term used in various ways, but the common
theme is that in one way or another, the end result is the
avoidance of an unwanted pregnancy. Quite often the
meaning may be a contraceptive device, such as a male or
female condom, cap or sponge. In this sense, the blocking
would be referring to the *emissions* of the male member. In
other cases the term could refer to behavior, style of dress or
any other characteristic that would render the *attentions* of a
male person less likely. Incidentally, I recently encountered
the phrase, "Dong Sarong" as a reference to a condom. I have
chosen not to include it as an entry in this book, as it does not
really meet the definition of a reduplicated phrase.

COMMUNITY IMMUNITY

This is a medical term referring to a situation where sufficient
individuals within a population are immune to a particular
disease, thereby making the spread of that disease slower
and/or less likely. A more common version of the expression
is, "herd immunity". Because most people rightly resent being
referred to as a "herd", bovine-fashion, by medical experts, the
more palatable variant, *community immunity*, is gaining
traction. The immunity of individuals within the community
may be genetic, but more commonly it is achieved through
vaccination. It is generally believed that 83 to 94 percent of
individuals in a population/herd need to be vaccinated to
bring about community immunity.

CRACK SHACK

A brothel. A potential remedy for *beaver-fever* for some of
those who use that latter term.

CRAY-CRAY

This is a term that engenders in me the characteristics that the term itself describes. It is a ridiculous expression that drives me absolutely *cray-cray*. It seems to have emerged around the year 2000, and implies craziness to the power of two, or craziness squared. Imagine my irritation when I saw the term on the wrapper of a "Snickers®" chocolate bar, part of an advertising campaign referenced elsewhere in this book (see *Drama Mama*).

CRINKLE-CRANKLE (CRINKUM-CRANKUM) WALL

A *crinkle crankle* wall, also known as a *crinkum crankum*, ribbon or serpentine wall is one that is built with a wavy, sinuous footprint. The design saves bricks because it can be a single brick thick, but still withstand expected winds without toppling, and with no need for buttresses. By far the greatest concentration of such walls is in the East Anglia region of England, and in particular within the county of Suffolk where at least 50 still exist. Many were built in the 1600s by Dutch drainage engineers as they converted the swampy fens of the region into usable farm land. The engineers referred to the walls as slangenmuur, meaning snake walls. In the United States, in the grounds of the University of Virginia, in Charlottesville, there are a number of crinkle crankle walls. These were installed at the request of Thomas Jefferson, founder of the university and third President of the country.

CRISS-CROSS

This refers to a pattern or design consisting of intersecting lines or bands. I met a real person with the name Christopher Cross a few years ago. Chris was indeed cross – with his parents - for bestowing upon him that name, and sentencing him to a life of recurring small talk and repetitive jokes from pretty much everyone, especially when meeting them for the first time.

CULTURE VULTURE

This term is defined in most dictionaries as referring to
someone who has an excessive or pretentious interest in the
arts. In my own mind, use of the word "vulture" always
conjures up images of the bird itself picking over the carcass of
a dead animal, usually resulting from road-kill. So to me,
when I hear the term *"culture vulture"* used in a fairly positive
sense, it seems odd. I suppose I should instead picture the
vulture soaring in the sky, constantly on the lookout for its
next object of interest. The term seems to have come into use
in the 1940s, possibly arising from lines in Ogden Nash's 1931
collection of poems *Free Wheeling*, "There is a vulture who
circles above the carcass of culture".

CURLY WURLY

Although in general I have not included many product names
as main entries in this book (while of course mentioning some
within discussion of the various terms), I can hardly fail to
mention "Curly Wurly®". This is a brand of chocolate bar
manufactured by Cadbury UK and sold in several countries. It
has a distinctive shape formed from three interwoven flat
strands of chocolate-coated caramel.

Cadbury made use of, but did not originate, the expression
curly wurly, which is a reduplicative form of curly originating
from the late 18th century.

DELHI BELLY

This is an example of how we often need to make light of
rather unpleasant illnesses or afflictions. In past days, when
the British Empire stretched across the globe, civil servants,
members of the armed forces, business people and their
families would often travel to, or even reside for lengthy
periods of time in, remote corners of the world. The food
available, and the methods of preparation, would frequently

mean that these people would be exposed to spices and benign micro-organisms that were new to them and could upset their digestive systems. The local people would be fully accustomed to the food, of course, and usually did not suffer any symptoms. The expatriate Britons on the other had would sometimes experience bouts of sickness, diarrhea and other unpleasant effects that might confine them to their beds for hours or days at a time. Because by far the greatest number of expatriate travels involved the Indian subcontinent, the term *Delhi belly* came to be used as a generic reference to upset stomachs of this type.

An equivalent non-reduplicative term is common in the United States, used to describe a similar affliction sometimes occurring during visits to Mexico, Central or South America. The term is "Montezuma's Revenge", alluding to the Aztec leader Montezuma II, 1466 – 1520, who was killed during the early part of the Spanish conquest of Mexico.

DIB-DAB

The act of dib-dabbing is to carry out a gentle sponging motion to, for example, mop up small spillages. One might *dib-dab* the surroundings of a minor scratch to remove blood before applying a sticky bandage. More appetizingly, many people incorrectly use the phrase to refer to the confectionary product "Dip dab®", manufactured by the British candy company Barratt. This delightful product takes the form of a small bag of sherbet powder which also contains a lollipop on a stick. The lollipop is repeated licked and dipped into the sherbet until the consumer has had their fill of sticky fizziness. Similar products from other global markets include "Pixy Stix®" and "Fun Dip®" manufactured by The Willy Wonka Candy Company, and Swizzels Matlow's "Double Dip®".

DIB-DOB

I have heard this term used to describe the action of rummaging around in a flower or vegetable bed in a garden. The origin may be associated with the implement used to plant seeds, namely a seed dibber (or dibbler, or dibble).

Also, the expression apparently was used at one time in the British military as a slang term for any foreign currency. (If so, I never heard it used.)

Perhaps more people would recognize the similar, "Dyb dyb dyb, dob dob dob" in the form of the Boy Scout/Brownie challenge/response chant, which was part of the, dob dob dob Grand Howl ceremony at one time. "Dyb" is an abbreviation for Do Your Best, and "Dob" for Do Our Best. Indeed, to this day when British adults are discussing the scouting movement, many will utter the expression, "Dib dib dib, dob dob dob" in a humorous way, with no idea what they are talking about. A former scout once told me that a parody version went as follows: "Dib dib dib: dob dob dob. Where's Akela? In the pub!"

DI-DO

To have a *di-do* is to jump around in an agitated or disorganized fashion, literally or figuratively, while undertaking a simple task, or in response to minor stress. Don't try searching for this term on-line, though. Around 99.9997 percent of search results will relate to the singer, "Dido".

DILLY-DALLY

Taking one's time to do something, probably to the frustration of, or at the expense of, other people can be referred to as *dilly-dally*ing. The likelihood that a particular individual will dilly-dally when sent on an errand can very often be predicted by those who know that person. The lines of the old music hall song, "My old man said: follow the van, and don't dilly-dally on the way!" illustrate this principle. The husband in the song assumed that his wife would dilly-dally while on her way to their new residence during their home move, and he was proved correct.

DING-DONG

"The couple next door were having a right old *ding-dong* again last night! If they keep this up I'll have to call the cops on them."

I'm not quite sure why a vociferous argument verging on violence would have acquired a label associated with the sound of a bell. Having said that, the practice sessions of the novice campanologists of one parish church near where I once lived did occasionally inflict auditory suffering upon me. After a few weeks I joined the bell-ringing team myself as a trainee. From that point forward, for the life of me I could not understand why any of the folks living within our musical footprint could possibly find anything unpleasant in our wonderful practices!

"Ding Dongs®" is the name of a brand of chocolate snack cakes produced and distributed in the United States by Hostess Brands. The cake is about the same size as an ice hockey puck. It is made of chocolate-covered chocolate sponge, with a creamy white filling. Produced since 1967, Ding Dongs were originally wrapped in metal foil so that they could be kept in lunch boxes without the chocolate melting.

A town in Texas is called Ding Dong. The Ding Dong mines form part of a UNESCO World Heritage Site in Cornwall.

Aside from its usages as discussed above, to some ears this phrase will almost certainly conjure-up mental images of scenes and the associated song from the movie *The Wizard of*

Oz, i.e., "Ding-dong the wicked witch is dead!" Somewhat cruelly, the song had a short-lived resurgence in the days following the death of the Right Honourable Margaret Thatcher, one of the more polarizing British Prime Ministers of the twentieth century. Admired for some for her tough stance against the Argentine military junta during the Falkland Islands conflict, but loathed by others for what were seen as draconian social and taxation policies, she remains a figure of very mixed image and legacy.

DINGLE-DANGLE

To *dingle-dangle* means to hang loosely, with the ability to swing back and forth. I have heard the term used to describe earrings, for example.

Some people may be familiar with the term from the rhyme/song called "Dingle Dangle Scarecrow". While many might assume this to be a traditional nursery rhyme, it was actually first published as "Wide Awake" in 1964 by Mills Music, London. The song was written by Mollie Russell-Smith and her brother Geoffry Russell-Smith. A board book for young children based on the song titled *I'm a Dingle Dangle Scarecrow*, written and illustrated by Annie Kubler, was published in 2003.

DITCH-WITCH®

This is trading name used by Charles Machine Works in the USA. The company manufactures various machines used in the construction industry to make sub-surface work easier, such as trenchers, horizontal drilling systems and the like. As with many trade names, the term Ditch Witch is now loosely and incorrectly used by many in the building trades to refer, generically, to any powered trenching machine.

DOWN-DOWN

A *down-down* is a ceremonial award, punishment or recognition carried out in a social gathering (involving alcoholic beverages) whereby an individual has to drink the entire contents of his or her glass without pausing. If the drinker does pause, or fails to finish the drink, then he or she must upend the remaining contents of the glass on top of their head. In former times, down-downs were fairly commonly doled-out at happy hours and at <u>*hash-bash*</u> events.

The 1974 song "Down Down" by the band Status Quo uses the word, "Down" 54 times in 35 lines of lyrics, with 13 occasions of the reduplicated term , "down down". For the 2019 Dr Phunk recording, "Down down down", well, go ahead and count the instances for yourself.

DOWNTOWN

This is a primarily American English term for the cultural or business heart of a city, often distinct from areas where most people actually live. Typically, people commute to *downtown* for work or to attend cultural or sporting events, but live in the suburbs. Any apartments or other residences that actually are located downton are usually very expensive. In British English it is more common to refer to the downtown district as the city center.

The 1964 Petula Clark song "Downtown" captures the sights, sounds and atmosphere of a typical downtown location in a catchy way.

DRAMA MAMA

In late 2015 an advertising campaign was launched by Mars, Inc. (the confectionery company) for the "Snickers®" candy bar. On the wrappers, the question, "Who are you when you're hungry?" was posed, and then answered with one of a number of short statements to describe the possible characteristics of a hungry person. One of the answers became mildly controversial in that the words, "Drama Mama" were considered by some to be sexist. Indeed, some of the other answers in the full list (Cranky, Rebellious, Feisty, Sleepy, Loopy, Goofball, Grouchy, Forgetful, Confused, Irritable, Drama Mama, Impatient, Complainer, Dramatic, Princess, Spacey, Whiny, Curmudgeon, Ornery, Testy and Snippy) also led to some raised eyebrows.

Anyway, "*drama mama*" certainly fits the definition of a reduplicated expression, and therefore deserves a place in this book. The term can be used to refer to a person who continually creates or attracts drama into their own life and that of others. Typically, a drama mama is overly emotional and sensitive, and is prone to overreacting to most events and circumstances. People of any gender can possess and display drama mama characteristics.

DUCKY LUCKY

See *Henny Penny* below, part of a family of similar terms peppered throughout this small tome.

EASY-PEASY

"Yes boss, I can do that. *Easy-peasy!*"

When something can be accomplished easily, or when a task was actually accomplished easily, the act of carrying out the task might be described as being easy-peasy.

The phrase brings to mind, for me at least, the old (1700s) rhyme, "Pease porridge hot, pease porridge cold, Pease porridge in the pot, nine days old; Some like it hot, some like it cold, Some like it in the pot, nine days old." This in turn begs the question as to what the heck "pease porridge" is. Well, it refers to a type of porridge or pudding made from peas, also known (in Middle English) as pease pottage. Interestingly "pease" was originally used as a mass noun, similar to the way the term "oatmeal" is used today. The singular word "pea" and the plural "peas" came about by back-formation.

EVEN-STEVEN(S)

This term is used to state that an arrangement is fair and equitable. Sometimes, it may imply that an earlier arrangement was unfair, but that the situation is now corrected. As an example, two people "going Dutch" for a night out might agree that one will pay for the taxi/Uber ride and the drinks, while the other will pay for the meal. A possible etymology of this term is from the obsolete use of the word, "Steven" to mean money. I also suspect that one of the uses of the word, "Steven" in Middle English, meaning, "promise", may have led in part to this reduplicated phrase.

FAG-HAG

A *fag-hag* is a heterosexual woman who takes delight in the social (only) company of homosexual men. The social dynamics of this situation go beyond my direct experience.

FAG-STAG

In similar vein to *fag-hag* above, the term *fag-stag* refers to a heterosexual man who has a circle of friends consisting mainly of homosexual men.

FAIR-AND-SQUARE

Fair and square implies that something, most likely a business deal, is straightforward and honest. Probably originating in the late sixteenth century, the phrase is reduplicative as well as tautological, as square at that time meant fair and honest. Terms such as square deal, square talk and others illustrate this meaning of square. There is speculation that the origin of square used in this way may be rooted in Freemasonry, or at least in the professions of stone masonry or carpentry. The similar term, "on the level", is also typically claimed to have such an origin. It is said that the first known printed use of the term fair and square was by Francis Bacon, who in 1604 wrote in his essay, *Of Prophecies*, "Faire, and square. The gamester calls fooles holy-day." (My own reading of the said essay does not show that line at all.)

In sports and other competitive endeavors, a team or individual might be beaten fair and square. In this sense the term implies that the opposition won by honest means, without cheating.

FANCY-SCHMANCY

If something is *fancy-schmancy*, it is probably perceived to be more ornate, or better turned out, than circumstances otherwise necessitate. Someone's choice of clothes for an informal gathering of friends might be way too fancy-schmancy, for example.

The "Schm...." formation as used in fancy-schmancy is relatively common within American Jewish English as a way of expressing emphasis, often in a somewhat disapproving way. Someone, for example, might ask, "Do you still smoke cigars?" The reply might be, "Smoke-schmoke! I gave that up last year, and now I can't even, stand the sight of a cigar!"

FIDDLE-FADDLE

In broad usage as a noun, *fiddle-faddle* can mean trivial, insignificant nonsense. It can also be a verb: someone might fiddle-faddle around rather than focus on the task at hand. In fact, I was fiddle-faddling around just a few minutes ago rather than concentrating on writing this paragraph.

Fiddle-Faddle is also a musical composition composed by Leroy Anderson, published on January 1, 1947, and premiered by Arthur on March 30, 1947 during a concert radio broadcast from the old Boston Opera House.

Possibly of greatest familiarity to those in the USA is the confection "Fiddle Faddle®", the candy-coated popcorn produced by ConAgra Foods. It was introduced in 1967. The popped popcorn is mixed with peanuts and is covered with caramel or toffee.

FISH-DISH

This is a rather juvenile term, relating to a specific course within an elaborate multi-course meal. In the example of the ridiculously-indulgent eleven-course meal described below, the Third Course might be referred to as the *fish-dish*. (In similar vein I have started to hear the "main course" of less elaborate meals referred to as "mains".)

The menu below is for the dinner served in the first-class dining saloon of the R.M.S. Titanic on April 14, 1912. Just a few hours later, after striking an iceberg, the ship sank during the early hours of April 15. The disaster claimed the lives of 1581 passengers and crew members.

First Course: Hors D'Oeuvres, Oysters. *Second Course*: Consommé Olga, Cream of Barley. *Third Course*: Poached Salmon with Mousseline Sauce, Cucumbers. *Fourth Course*: Filet Mignons Lili, Sauté of Chicken, Lyonnaise, Vegetable Marrow Farci. *Fifth Course*: Lamb, Mint Sauce; Roast Duckling, Apple Sauce; Sirloin of Beef; Chateau Potatoes, Green Peas, Creamed Carrots, Boiled Rice, Parmentier & Boiled New Potatoes. *Sixth Course*: Punch Romaine. *Seventh Course*: Roast Squab & Cress. *Eighth Course*: Cold Asparagus Vinaigrette. *Ninth Course*: Pate de Foie Gras, Celery. *Tenth Course*: Waldorf Pudding, Peaches in Chartreuse Jelly, Chocolate & Vanilla Eclairs, French Ice

Cream. *Eleventh Course*: Fresh Fruits & Cheese, Coffee, Port
& Other Distilled Spirits.

FLIM-FLAM

Most commonly this term would be followed by the word,
"artist". A *flim-flam* artist is a person who engages in
deception, usually for personal gain, who might also be
described as a fraudster, trickster or con-man/woman.

FLIP-FLAP

The movement of something that flaps or flops about might be
described as *flip-flap*ping. Also, a move in football (soccer)
whereby a player fools another into thinking that the ball is
going in one direction, where really the player intends to move
in another, is known as the flip-lap. The move was brought to
prominence in the 1960s by the Japanese-Brazilian football
player Sérgio Echigo.

FLIP-FLOP

Among the many common uses of this term, the most
entertaining is the one that is used to describe the actions of
politicians. For reasons that defy logic, at least in my view, it
is generally perceived to be a weakness if a politician changes
his or her mind on a topic. Doing so is derided as *flip-flop*ping
by members of the media, and by the political opponents of
the flip-flopper. I suppose the prevailing view is that
politicians should form opinions and never, ever, change
them. How strange, in such a fast-paced and complex world,
that flexibility, adaptability and agility are seen to be character
flaws.

FOD-PLOD

"Corporal Smith, take five of these people loafing around
playing uckers in the crew room, and do a *fod-plod* on Pan 7!"
38

Yes, I realize that the example requires elucidation! "FOD" is a term used in many air forces and aviation organizations to refer the items that can cause "Foreign Object Damage" to aircraft engines and structures. A piece of FOD, sucked into an engine intake, can cause catastrophic damage. As a result, frequent physical walks of aircraft dispersal areas need to be undertaken to ensure that litter, dropped pieces of wire, or any other potentially hazardous items are collected and removed. Certainly, sweeper trucks are used, but around aircraft dispersals there is often a considerable amount of ground equipment (stairs, power trolleys, towing arms, chocks, etc.) that impede the movement of vehicles. So the human eye and hand are needed to supplement the actions of the vehicular brush. In addition, the act of performing a FOD-plod is character building in the extreme.

I have also heard this essential activity referred to as a "FOD walk", but I must say that not only is the term fod-plod more musical in sound, but it also deftly captures the somewhat monotonous nature of the task.

As for the word "uckers" I used in my example at the start of this entry, that's what the game, *Ludo* is called in the British Royal Air Force and other branches of the British military. The rules of uckers are slightly different from those of the civilian Ludo.

FRIGHT NIGHT

Especially on the run-up to Halloween, a *fright night* is a party or gathering that has a horror theme to the festivities. Many social clubs, and sometimes businesses, will host fright nights.

FUDDY-DUDDY

Some might say that reading a book like this is conclusive proof that the person doing so is a *fuddy-duddy*. The term implies that someone is dull, uninteresting and unexciting,

with little interest in current culture, memes and trends. Au
contraire!

FUNKY-MONKEY

A number of businesses and products have taken variations on
the phrase *Funky Monkey* as their name. There is also the
2004 family comedy movie called *Funky Monkey* starring
Matthew Modine, Seth Adkins and Roma Downey. It was
written by Lance Kinsey and Peter Nelson. The director was
Harry Basil. The movie was released direct-to-video, with no
theatrical release.

FUNNY MONEY

Typically, this expression describes counterfeit paper
currency. By extension it can also refer to a payment
arrangement involving illicitly-acquired funds generally, or
funds which turn out not to have zero value when attempts are
made to cash-in those funds. Pyramid selling schemes and
Ponzi schemes are examples of get-rich-quick arrangements
that generate supposed vast returns, but which essentially
generate only *funny money*. Caveat emptor!

FUZZY-WUZZY

Fuzzy-Wuzzy was a bear, Fuzzy-Wuzzy had no hair! So Fuzzy-
Wuzzy wasn't fuzzy, wuz 'e? That's how the rhyme goes that
many people may remember from childhood. As such, the
usage is relatively innocent and innocuous.

In a rather more derogatory way, the term, "Fuzzy-Wuzzy" was
used by British colonial soldiers to refer to the 19th-century
Beja warriors who supported the Sudanese Mahdi in the
Mahdist War of 1881 to 1899.

Returning to the poem, a friend of mine once told me that his
mother devised and added several lines. The only ones I can

recall are, "Fuzzy-Wuzzy got his crop, at the North Pole barber's shop!" Unrelatedly, I also recall someone who was part of that circle of friends who, not being able to afford a new van for his business, had to settle for a rather battered second-hand van. He called it his, "van ordinaire".

GEEK-SPEAK

A mildly derogatory term for the type of technology-related terminology used liberally and frequently by those having a geeky fascination with all things technological. I recently came across the related expression, "Geekumentary", used to describe broadcast or streaming non-fiction documentaries.

GENDER-BENDER

A person who flouts or challenges traditional concepts of gender, especially with respect to conventional forms of behavior or dress, might be referred to as a *gender-bender*. Depending on who is using the term and the circumstances at the time, the expression could be pejorative, or it might be expressing approval.

GEORGIE-PORGIE

"*Georgie-Porgie* pudding and pie, kissed the girls and made them cry. When the boys came out to play, Georgie Porgie ran away." That's how I remember the nursery rhyme that I learnt as a child. Even at the time I found it unsettling. Today, the overtones and implications of unwarranted, uninvited amorous attention would raise many eyebrows.

Many theories suggest that the rhyme is an allusion to real historical events or people, but none can be proven. Candidates include George Villiers, 1st Duke of Buckingham (1592–1628), Charles II (reigned from 1660 to 1685) and George I (reigned from 1714 to 1727). In Scotland, some hold that the rhyme is of Jacobite origin, referring to the flight of

George II to mainland Europe as the Jacobite armies advanced during the rebellion of 1745. At least once I have heard that the historical person referenced was George IV. Some hold that the rhyme describes the Great Fire of London which started in Pudding Lane and by some accounts ended at Pye Corner. The belief in this case is that "the boys" could be a reference to the firefighters, with Georgie Porgie being the arsonist. This seems rather far-fetched, especially as "the girls" would still need explanation.

GOOSEY LOOSEY

See _Henny Penny_ below, part of a family of similar terms peppered throughout this small tome.

GO-SLOW

Growing up in the 1960s and 70s in Britain, I became accustomed to the main evening TV news broadcasts being seemingly totally devoted to coverage of industrial action and labour disputes. Just about every major manufacturer, and most national industries, were plagued with strikes, sit-ins, work-to-rule action and _go-slows_. The workers in these organizations had many genuine grievances over pay and conditions of work. Conversely, their employers were trying to balance costs, productivity and profits. It seemed as though immovable objects were being impacted by unstoppable forces. Some groups of workers took the ultimate action of strikes, or imposed work stoppages. Others took a milder confrontational approach by working to the letter of their employment contracts or union agreements. No, "going the extra mile" or injection of good will was extended during these work-to-rule events. A similar tactic was to work with the minimum level of energy, and at the slowest pace possible, without breaching current agreements, thereby impacting productivity. This approach was described as a go-slow.

It does seem now, some 50 years later, that the general level of cooperation between workers and management in Britain is higher. Surely that is a good thing?

HAIRY-SCARY

Something which is frightening to the extent that one's body hair may stand on end in response (thereby causing goose-bumps or goose-pimples) might be described as *hairy-scary*.

Hairy Scary is also a French animated television series, directed by Rudi Bloss/Wolf-Ruediger Bloss, created by Jan Rijsselberge and co-produced by Alphanim.

The *Casper and the Angels* television series created by Hanna-Barbera productions has a charter named Hairy Scary.

I have also heard the term, used disparagingly, to refer to people having an unexpected level of hirsuteness in areas of the body where hair would normally be found in less abundance.

HANDY-DANDY

"Having trouble untying the knots in that rope? Here, use the awl in my *handy-dandy* pocket knife."

This expression implies that a useful object is easily available, probably in the possession of, or very close to, the speaker, and that it will be very efficacious in whatever challenge or task is being attempted. There is a slight air of smugness associated with the use of the term! The speaker is letting the listener know that the speaker thought ahead, and invested time and possibly money in preparing for the very situation where this handy-dandy object is now needed. Further, the speaker is implying that the listener is less than fully prepared, and should also have thought ahead, just like the smug speaker. Am I being paranoid here? Apparently, some people think I am!

HANKLYN-JANKLIN

Hanklyn-Janklin: A stranger's rumble-tumble guide to some words, customs, and quiddities, Indian and Indo-British is a book authored in 1992 by Nigel B. Hankin. The title contains a reduplicated expression (*Hanklyn-Janklin*) in honor of the 1886 predecessor work, <u>Hobson-Jobson</u>, discussed later in this book. The *Hanklyn-Janklin* book is a glossary of Indian English expressions, and of words originating from Indian languages that are now current in mainstream English.

HANKY-PANKY

Illicit or dubious behavior, possibly of a sexual or legally questionable kind, could be called *hanky-panky*. The light-hearted sound and resonance of this term mean that it would be an unsuitable label for activities that are severe in nature. Rather, it tends to be used for milder shenanigans.

HAPPY CHAPPY

Most often this expression would be preceded by the words, "not a". An example of usage might involve a scenario where someone is explaining how another person felt after some detrimental circumstance was imposed upon them. "John found out yesterday that his company has cancelled all summer vacation because of project slippages. He was not a *happy chappy*. He had just paid a non-refundable booking deposit for a safari holiday to Namibia!"

HAPPY-CLAPPY

Church attendance in several European countries has been declining for many years. Mainstream churches in particular have seen congregations dwindle. The Church of England is no exception to this trend. In response, various different strategies have been adopted, diocese by diocese and parish by parish. Some assumed that the traditional nature of worship was to blame, and attempted to "modernize" by bringing in what they perceived to be more contemporary music and musical instruments. Thundering pipe organs and hymns of old were replaced with guitars and less intellectually-demanding lyrics. Others in the Church decided that, rather than moving to a lower common denominator, a better approach would be to double-down on the spiritual value of traditional forms and styles of worship. This latter group, somewhat disdainfully, often refer to the contemporary services as *happy-clappy* events.

HARLEY FARLEY

In addition to being the real name of many different individuals, *Harley Farley* is a character in a series of children's books by Donna Munoz. The first in the series was the 2014 volume, *Harley Farley's First Halloween: A Zombie Book (Harley Farley Zombie Books 1)*.

HARUM-SCARUM

Used as an adverb or noun, *harum-scarum* refers to behavior or to a person that is reckless, irresponsible or foolhardy. Originating from as early as 1751, the etymology seems to come from *hare*, meaning to harass, plus *scare*.

In 1965 a musical comedy movie called *Harum Scarum* was released starring Elvis Presley. The UK title was *Harem Holiday*.

HASH-BASH

One of the legacies of colonial-era history is the existence of running/social clubs called "Hash House Harriers" in various parts of the world. The practice of hashing originated in 1938 in Selayang Quarry, Selangor, in what was then known as the Federated Malay States, now the country of Malaysia. A group of British colonial officers and expatriates began meeting at weekly intervals, on a Monday, to hold running events in the form of a traditional British paper chase, commonly referred to as a "hare and hounds" run. The aim was to use exercise to shake off the effects of the overindulgence of the preceding weekend.

Today, *the* Hash House Harriers (HHH or sometimes H3) is an international group of non-competitive running social clubs. Modern H3 groups exist worldwide. An event is known as a hash or a hash run or simply hashing. Typically at a hash, one or more members, known as "hares", lay a trail. The rest of the group, the "pack" or the "hounds", follow the trail, running or walking as their individual abilities permit. Traditionally, torn paper was used as the trail marker, but with greater sensitivity to litter and pollution, less obtrusive, biodegradable materials are now more common. Today, flour sawdust or chalk are mostly used to mark the trail.

Sometimes, members describe their H3 group as "a drinking club with a running problem." This is because for many members, the social and beer component of an event is of equal importance to the athletic component. After most hashes, members gather at a club house or other establishment where beer can be consumed in appropriate quantities. Such a gathering would typically be called a *hash-bash*.

HASH-CASH

The term used to describe membership dues or event fees charged by some Hash House Harrier groups (see previous item). By extension, the club treasurer may also go by the nickname/title, *Hash-Cash*.

HASTY TASTY

In Dayton, Ohio, USA an American diner-style restaurant called the *Hasty Tasty* Pancake House has been in business for many years.

The name of the restaurant always makes me think of hasty pudding, a traditional dish originating in British cuisine and dating from at least the sixteenth century. It consists of wheat flour boiled in milk or water until it becomes a thick batter. Usually a variety of additional ingredients are added, such as sugar, cream, butter, breadcrumbs, currants, raisins or eggs. After colonial settlers moved to North America, the lack of some traditional ingredients led to variations of hasty pudding that used alternatives such as corn, oats, molasses, maple syrup and salted meat, with names such as Indian Mush, Indian Pudding, Nasaump, and Corn Mush. Hasty pudding itself is even mentioned in a verse from an early version of the song, Yankee Doodle: "Fath'r and I went down to camp, Along with Captain Goodin', And there we saw the men and boys, As thick as hasty puddin'".

I also feel obliged to mention The Hasty Pudding Theatricals, known informally as The Pudding. Formed in 1795, it is a student theatrical society at Harvard University. One of the society's staples is its burlesque cross-dressing musicals.

HEEBIE JEEBIES

This term describes a feeling of fear, foreboding or revulsion engendered by circumstances, people, places or objects. "Just the look of that guy gives me the *heebie jeebies!*" In terms of origin of the phrase, although it may well have been used orally previously, the first know printed occurrence seems to be from 1923 with the spelling "heeby jeebys". It appeared in the newspaper *New York American*, 26 October 1923 as part of the comic strip *Barney Google* by U.S. cartoonist Billy De Beck.

HELTER-SKELTER

This is a term used in the UK for large slides in fairgrounds/funfairs: the type where a helical slide descends around the outside of a central tower. Riders are usually given a sisal front door mat to sit on as they slide down the ride. By extension, the term *helter-skelter* is used to refer to a fast, near-uncontrolled, form of running. "He ran helter-skelter down the street to try to get to the station before his train pulled away from the platform."

HENNY PENNY

If you have been skim-reading or sherbet-dabbing the entries in this book, you may have noticed that several of them point forwards or backwards to this entry. *Henny Penny* is one common title for a folk tale which, possibly more commonly, goes by the name of Chicken Little or sometimes Chicken Licken. In the tale, the main character, a chick, believes that the world is coming to an end when an acorn falls on his head because, "The sky is falling". The chick decides to warn the King, and on his journey to do so meets many other animals, with names such as Henny Penny or Hen-Len, Cocky Locky, Ducky Lucky or Ducky Daddles, Drakey Lakey, Gander Lander, Goosey Loosey or Goosey Poosey, Foxy Woxy or Foxy Loxy, Turkey Lurkey and others. I won't spoil the story by revealing an ending. There are in fact many variations of the ending.

As a folk tale the story goes back at least 25 centuries as an oral tradition. An early printed version was published by Just Matthias Thiele in Danish in 1823, with character names that included Hone Pone, Gaase Paase, Raev Skraev and Kylling Kluk.

HEYDAY

This term is included as an example of how some expressions or words come to be seen as based on reduplication, when in fact that was not originally the case. *Heyday* was originally used as an interjection, much like its derivative "hey!" is today. It came also to mean high spirits, as in Shakespeare's *Hamlet*, Act III, Scene IV, where the Prince of Denmark tells his mother, "You cannot call it love; for at your age, The heyday in the blood is tame." Starting around the eighteenth century the current meaning of heyday, a period in time when someone or something was at its greatest prominence or popularity, emerged. This was probably due to people assuming that the "day" syllable meant the same as the individual word day, a period of twenty four hours.

HIGGLEDY-PIGGLEDY

Usage examples: "The houses in that subdivision are laid out all *higgledy-piggledy*, with no rhyme or reason." "The papers on John's desk are all higgledy-piggledy"."

A term used to describe disorder, confusion, or lack of planning. Some may also remember a nursery rhyme that runs as follows: "Higgledy Piggledy, My fat hen, She lays eggs for gentlemen; Sometimes nine, And sometimes ten, Higgledy Piggledy, My fat hen!" I have also seen the rhyme with "black hen" instead of "fat hen". In the rhyme, I suspect the name Higgledy Piggledy for the hen is a reference to the likely way she has to deposit the vast quantity of eggs described. Maybe two or three eggs can be arranged with care, but nine or ten presents a challenge!

HI-FI

At one time, it seemed that someone's social standing was directly related to the cost and/or capabilities of the *hi-fi* system that was present in their home, college room or bedroom. Hi-fi was the term used to describe a "high fidelity" audio system, typically consisting of a turntable to play vinyl records, an amplifier, a radio tuner and possibly a dual cassette tape player. All of this equipment would be stacked vertically, possible in a custom-built rack, and would be connected to two or more powerful speakers. As with all technology, one could buy a basic set-up for an affordable price, or pour hundreds or thousands of dollars or pounds into a system perceived to be "high-end". In later years, the moves to compact discs, then to MP3-style digital files, and then to streaming music, have led to hi-fi systems of the traditional type becoming very rare indeed. All of that said, there remains an enthusiastic group of vinyl record aficionados who are insistent that the sound quality available from a pressed analog recording is more natural than is possible from a purely digital medium. Ironically, in most homes today, streaming music is delivered via _Wi-Fi_!

HIKEY-BOKEY

When I first heard my wife use this term, I assumed that it was fairly commonly used in the United States, or at least in the South. On further research I believe her family to be the actual originators! She remembers sitting in her grandfather's mountain cabin in the Smoky Mountains listening to him tell stories to her and her cousins during family gatherings. Gathered around the fire on a windy night he would sometimes relate, "Listen to the wind! When it moans around the house like that, wooo-wooo-WOOO, you know a little boy has been bad. When it whistles some more, wooo-wooo-WOOO, you know a little girl has been bad. Quiet now, and listen. Shush. Listen. What is that?" Then, after a pause, he would shout, _Hikey Bokey_!! And of course, at that point the children, whose eyes had been getting rounder and rounder, would jump out of their chairs! In this usage, Hikey Bokey referred to a Boogie Man type of entity.

HOB-NOB

To *hob-nob* means to associate with one or more people in friendly or familiar terms, often implying that such association is outside the norm in some way. One might be accused of inappropriately hobnobbing with people of a higher or lower social standing than oneself, for example. A group of ex-patriate workers might frown on one of their number for, "hob-nobbing with the locals".

An obsolete usage of the term was to utter it as a toast while touching glasses, the equivalent of saying, "cheers" today. The derivation seems to be from, "hob and nob", or perhaps, "hob or nob", which may have meant to give and take, i.e. taking turns buying rounds of drinks. An earlier dialectical version was hab nab, to have or have not, when inviting someone to have a drink.

As a closing note on this entry, I feel compelled to mention "HobNobs®", a brand of biscuit/cookie made by McVities, and marketed in the United Kingdom and several other countries since 1985.

HOBSON-JOBSON

The book, *Hobson-Jobson: A Glossary of Colloquial Anglo-Indian Words and Phrases, and of Kindred Terms, Etymological, Historical, Geographical and Discursive* was first published in 1865, written by Sir Henry Yule and Arthur Coke Burnell. The book is a dictionary of many Anglo-Indian words and terms from Indian languages which came into use during British rule in India. (See also the entry for <u>Hanklyn-Janklin</u> earlier in this book).

In linguistics, the "law of Hobson-Jobson" refers to the process of phonological change whereby words, loaned from one language into another, become adapted to the phonology of the receiving language.

HOCUS-POCUS

If someone is making use of *Hocus Pocus*, they are using deceptive language or actions designed to divert attention from the true facts of a situation. The origin of the term is from stage magic shows, where the art of misdirection is an essential component of sleight-of-hand and other illusions.

An alternate term, and possibly the original term, for sleight-of-hand is legerdemain. The earliest known English-language work on magic was published in 1635 with the title, *Hocus Pocus Junior: The Anatomie of Legerdemain*. The author was anonymous, but it is possible that it was written by Hocus Pocus, which was the stage name of a magician of the era. A magician from that period named William Vincent was granted a license to perform magic in England in 1619. Whether this person was Hocus Pocus, and whether Hocus Pocus did indeed write the book mentioned, is not certain.

An alternate etymological theory for the phrase is that it derives from a corruption of the Latin used in the Roman Catholic Mass, *Hoc est enim corpus meum*, meaning, "This is my body". Some credence is lent to this by the fact that in other countries, additional words are added after Hocus Pocus as part of the magician's chant that also may originate from the Mass or from the Credo. Examples include "Pilatus pas" in the Netherlands, perhaps taken from, *sub Pontius Pilato passus et sepultus es"*, meaning, "He suffered under Pontius Pilate and was buried". Also, in Scandinavia and Russia, the word filiokus is sometimes added, a corruption of the term *filioque*, "and from the Son".

Yet another suggested origin is from Norse folklore, where a magician/demon of the North was named Ochus Bochus.

HODGE-PODGE

Usage example: "Did you see that new concept car on the news? I didn't care for it. The front end looks like a truck, the back end slopes like an old Mach 1 Mustang, and they slapped a gull-wing door on the driver's side and left a normal door for the passenger. What a *hodge-podge!*"

A hodge-podge is thus a hybrid mixture of items that don't necessarily work as a coherent whole, or, if they do, it is a rather surprising that they do so. One might suspect a culinary origin for such a term, and indeed one would be correct. As a dish, a Hodge-Podge is a soup or stew made of a mixture of various ingredients. In Victorian times the term was also a name for a very specific soup called <u>Hotch-Potch</u>, a thick mutton soup with pieces of meat and all sorts of vegetables. Lancashire <u>Hot-Pot</u> is another variant.

HO HOS

Ho Hos are small chocolate snack cakes produced by Hostess Brands. They take the form of a chocolate-covered, rolled spiral cylinder of chocolate sponge cake, with a layer of cream inside. Generic cakes of this type would probably be called mini Swiss rolls. It is believed that the first Ho Hos were produced in a San Francisco bakery around the year 1920. A cartoon mascot for Ho Hos called "Happy Ho Ho®" was used on the boxes, and appeared in print ads and in television commercials for many years starting from the 1970s. He wore clothes similar to those of Robin Hood, and had a body shaped like a Ho Ho cake.

HOI-POLLOI

This is a disdainful term used by those who consider themselves to be members of the social, intellectual or financial "upper classes". It is a way of describing the ninety five percent of the population that the users of the term deem to be beneath their contempt. Equivalent expressions include, "the great unwashed", "plebs", "proles", "the masses" and "sheeple". The term comes directly from Ancient Greek, where *hoi polloi* meant, "the many", and was used in a positive way, reflecting admiration for democracy. The contrasting term, *hoi oligoi*, meaning "the few", is the root of the term "oligarchy".

HOITY-TOITY

It is rather interesting that this term immediately follows <u>hoi-polloi</u> in this book, as it is used in a reverse-disdainful way by those who might be described as <u>hoi-polloi</u> themselves. *Hoity-toity* means snobbish, disdainful, self-infatuated, pretentious, etc. It originates from an obsolete sixteenth century word, "hoit", which meant to play the fool or act in a frivolous manner, which some aristocrats may have been prone to do. (An incorrect etymology of the term is doing the rounds on social media, where the origin is said to derive from the French <u>haut toit</u>, meaning, "high roof".)

HOKEY-COKEY / HOKEY-POKEY / HOKEY-TOKEY

These are variations on the name of a participation dance popular in many parts of the English-speaking world. *Hokey-cokey* in the UK, *Hokey-pokey* in the USA, Canada, Australia, Ireland, Israel and the Caribbean, and *Hokey-tokey* in New Zealand, are all descendants of British folk dances common around the early 1800s. Just as the name varies, the words and actions of the dance differ slightly country to country. The (frequently alcohol-fueled) UK variant involves dancing and actions to coincide with the following words: "You put your [left arm] in, your [left arm] out: in, out, in, out, you shake it all about. You do the hokey cokey, and you turn around. That's what it's all about!" There is also a chorus, where the dancers rush in to the center of the dance floor in unison, singing, "Whoa-oh, the hokey cokey, whoa-oh the hokey cokey, whoa-oh the hokey cokey, knees bend arms stretch, ra! ra! ra!"

HOLY MOLY / HOLY MOLEY

This is an expression of surprise, similar to "Holy Cow", which many people will associate with the *Batman* TV series of the 1960s. Batman's sidekick, Robin, (played by Burt Ward) delivered 369 such exclamations. Robin's terms were almost always specific to a particular plot point or event in an episode, and in addition to *Holy Moly* included such gems as, "Holy Cliffhangers", "Holy Polar Ice Sheet", "Holy Known Unknown Flying Objects" and "Holy Non-Sequiturs". Despite all of this usage by Robin, the first comic character to use Holy Moly was Captain Marvel, star of a comic strip written by Bill Parker and C. C. Beck starting in the 1940s. The phrase was Captain Marvel's customary expression of surprise. It, and the magic phrase, "Shazam!" that radio reporter Billy Batson had to say in order to transform into Captain Marvel, entered popular culture. The first documented print use of the term "Holey Moley" is older still, though. It appeared in the book, *Running It Off or Hard Hit: An Enthralling Story of Racing, Love and Intrigue*, by Nathaniel Gould, published in 1892 by George Routledge and Sons. The book, re-issued by John Long Ltd in 1919, included the following passage: "Whew!" he whistled, softly; "that's curious. Same name as the lady at our place. Suppose he should be her husband. Holy moley, what a game. I've made a discovery. I must take particular of this man. He'll come in useful I reckon."

HONKY-TONK

It is hard for me to use this term, or to write about it, without the song, "Honky Tonk Women" by the Rolling Stones coming to mind. For others, the term may trigger different memories, as it has appeared in many different guises in popular culture.

A honky-tonk is an establishment, usually a bar, which offers country music entertainment, often in a style that is itself referred to as honky-tonk. This style today features steel guitar and fiddle. There is usually a rhythm section which plays a two-beat rhythm and a backbeat.

The original honky-tonk style was primarily performed on a piano in ragtime style, but with melody being less important than rhythm. In part, this was because pianos were often less well maintained than they deserved to be, typically being out of tune more than in tune. Early honky-tonk was a major influence on the style of piano playing known as _boogie-woogie_, as demonstrated by *Honky Tonk Music*, recorded by Jelly Roll Morton in 1938.

HOO-HA

The most common use of this term is to describe a commotion, an uproar, a brouhaha, a hullabaloo, or other animated behaviour or discussion. There might be a massive *hoo-ha* in the news media about something controversial that a politician or celebrity has said, for example. Often, a hoo-ha will die down in time, possibly because an altogether new hoo-ha about another topic entirely rises to the fore. With the meaning just stated, hoo-ha dates to at least as early as the 1930s, and may have come from the Yiddish *hu-ha*, used in a similar fashion and also as a general exclamation of surprise.

Another meaning of hoo-ha is as a euphemism for vagina.

HOOTY-HOOT

A term used by a very lovely woman, when she was a child, to refer to an owl.

HOOTY-TOOTY

In the Southern United States, this is a more common variant of the term _hoity-toity_. The fact that the words hooty and tooty both rhyme with the word snooty make this a better variant in many ways.

HOTCH-POTCH

(A variation of the term _hodge-podge_ discussed earlier, used in the same way.)

HOT POT

This is almost exclusively a purely culinary term, most commonly occurring as part of the name of the dish, Lancashire _Hot Pot_, or Hotpot. (See also the earlier listing for _hodge podge_). The classic Lancashire Hot Pot is made traditionally from lamb or mutton with onions, all topped with sliced potatoes. It is left to bake in the oven for many hours in a heavy pot and on a low heat, until the potato covering is lightly browned.

HOT-SPOT

Figuratively, a _hot-spot_ is any location where some kind of activity is concentrated, or is happening at a greater frequency that at other locations. A particular part of a city might be described as a hot-spot for drug-dealing or prostitution, for example.

Geological hot spots are locations in the Earth's upper mantle where hot magma from the lower mantle has welled-up, and is likely to develop volcanic characteristics. On the Earth's surface, geographical hot spots are locations where the temperature is warmer than surrounding areas, possibly due to terrain features or other microclimate effects. On an organism's skin, including that of people and pets, a hot-spot is an area of infected, inflamed skin.

In technological parlance, a _Wi-Fi_ hot-spot is a location where users of wireless devices can connect to the internet.

HOTSIE-TOTSIE

This expression, often spelled as hotsy-totsy, seems to have a variety of meanings. Firstly, it was at one time used to describe something as being normal, stable, very acceptable, about as right as it could possibly be. "Things were pretty dicey in the passenger cabin for a while there with all the air turbulence, but now it's all *hotsie-totsie*". More recently, the term implies that something is an especially good, superlative, example of its category. Someone might be known for the hotsie-totsie car they drive, for example. And this leads us to perhaps the most current use of the expression.

More and more in life, people are primarily judged on their looks and sexual attractiveness. It is a hugely coveted characteristic to be able to be described as "hot". All genders can be hot, or not. So if someone is a real hotsie-totsie, they possess exceptional hotness. To be frank, I find the current obsession with hotness, and the use of the word hot to characterize selected people, to be overworked and tiresome. Ironically, just a few years ago, being cool was as desirable a characteristic as being hot is now. The addition of totsie as the second part of the phrase, aside from pure reduplication, may also allude to the word totty. In British English, totty is used to refer to sexually attractive women, considered collectively. An individual woman within this category would be referred to as a bit of totty.

HUBBA BUBBA

"Hubba Bubba®" is a brand of bubble gum. The gum was originally produced by the Wm. Wrigley Jr. Company, a subsidiary of Mars, Inc. Initially, production and availability of the gum was limited to the USA. It is now produced in many additional countries, and is available in the form of a "tape" roll as well as in more traditional chunk/chew format.

HUBBA-HUBBA

One of my treasured possessions as a teenager was a T-shirt that a friend brought me from the USA. The shirt was emblazoned with a caricature of a chopper-riding motorcyclist, a typical hippy biker, and the phrase, "*Hubba-hubba*, burn dat rubba" was printed above the picture. At the time I assumed the phrase hubba-hubba was purely a reference to the sound made by a v-twin motorcycle similar to the one on the shirt. (Actually of course, such engines emit the sound, "*potato-potato*".)

More recently I realized that hubba-hubba was often used as an expression of delight, surprise, appreciation or admiration with regard to the appearance or qualities of an object or person that is considered appealing or desirable. "Look at that amazing *zoot-suit*! Hubba-hubba!" By extending the meaning to include a shout of delight made while enjoying something, a 2004 New Zealand "safe sex" health campaign included the words, "No Rubba, no Hubba-Hubba!".

HUBBLE BUBBLE

An onomatopoeic expression used to describe the boiling of a substance. Also, the sound made by hookah pipe. Where I have heard this expression used most often, though, is as part of a *mis*quotation of Shakespeare. "Hubble, bubble, toil and trouble" is frequently uttered by people for no apparent reason, possibly when they are witnessing or anticipating some sort of difficulty. In fact, the actual lines from the Song of the Witches in *Macbeth* are, "Double, double toil and trouble; Fire burn and cauldron bubble."

HUEY, DEWEY and LOUIE

The nephews of Donald Duck, who appear in some of his cartoons.

HUMPTY DUMPTY

I mentioned *Humpty Dumpty* in passing as part of the entry
<u>Anguish Languish</u> earlier, but of course Humpty Dumpty
deserves its (his?) own entry.

Many people will be familiar with the nursery rhyme that goes
as follows: "Humpty Dumpty sat on a wall, Humpty Dumpty
had a great fall. All the King's horses and all the King's men,
couldn't put Humpty together again."

So what was Humpty Dumpty? Typically he is depicted as an
egg with facial features, legs and arms, dressed in clothes that
might be appropriate for a child in Georgian times. The rhyme
seems to have first appeared in the late eighteenth century.
Words have varied over the years. A version from 1797 went,
"Humpty Dumpty sat on a wall, Humpty Dumpty had a great
fall. Four-score Men and Four-score more, Could not make
Humpty Dumpty where he was before."

As with many nursery rhymes, there are various theories as to
possible true historical or political underpinnings that gave
rise to the rhyme. In the case of Humpty Dumpty, one theory
is that it was simply a riddle, with the solution being that
Humpty Dumpty was an egg. Others believe that the rhyme
was a reference to King Richard the Third of England, or to a
siege engine, or possibly to a canon, used during the English
Civil War.

The disintegration of Humpty Dumpty has been used as an
illustration of the Second Law of Thermodynamics, whereby a
system can increase in entropy (disorganization), but not
(normally) decrease.

Humpty Dumpty appeared as a character in the book *Through
the Looking-Glass* by Lewis Carroll (1871), where he enters
into a discussion on semantics with Alice. The interaction
between Alice and Humpty Dumpty regarding the meaning of

words, and one's right (or lack of) to use words to have whatever meaning one wishes, has been quoted in a number of landmark legal proceedings in the UK and the USA.

HURDY-GURDY

A *hurdy-gurdy* is a stringed musical instrument. It makes use of a hand-turned, rosined wheel that rubs against the strings to produce sounds, pretty much in the same way as a violin bow. Individual notes played on the instrument therefore sound much like those of a violin. The hurdy-gurdy additionally has a keyboard that is used to play melodies. The keyboard functions by pressing small wooden wedges, called tangents, against the strings to change their pitch. Like most other acoustic stringed instruments, it has a sound board and hollow cavity to make the vibration of the strings audible.

From the above, one can clearly deduce that a hurdy-gurdy is far from being a simple instrument, and considerable skill is needed to play it. Sadly, there does seem to be a perception that the instrument requires very <u>little</u> musical ability to play. Many people, wrongly, assume that turning the handle is all that is required. Perhaps they think there is some magical mechanical wizardry going on inside the sound box? In any event, players of the instrument, known as hurdy-gurdy men, have been traditionally portrayed in popular culture as semi-skilled individuals.

Notwithstanding the above, the term hurdy-gurdy was also used in the eighteenth century to refer to a portable barrel organ or street organ. Such instruments *did* only require the turning of a crank to play them. In that case, the player, sometimes called an organ-grinder, did not need to possess musical skill. The music itself was usually coded onto rolls of paper or onto pins on a rotating barrel.

Many people will know of the instrument from its extensive mentions in the song, "Hurdy Gurdy Man" recorded by the singer Donovan in April 1968. An earlier song of the same name was recorded by the band The Spectres, a predecessor to the band Status Quo, in 1966.

HURLY-BURLY

A *hurly burly* is an uproar, a commotion, a tumult. It implies a noisy, busy, confrontational environment. In this sense, the term was used by Shakespeare in *Macbeth*, Act 1, Scene 1: First Witch: "When shall we three meet again / In thunder, lightning, or in rain?" Second Witch: "When the hurlyburly's done, / When the battle's lost and won." This use by Shakespeare provided inspiration for the selection of the title *Hurlyburly* for a 1984 dark comedy play by David Rabe, which was subsequently produced as a movie.

One synonym for hurly burly is hubbub, which is itself a near-reduplicative term. Hubbub refers to a chaotic noise or uproar caused by a crowd of people. (I have also personally witnessed turkeys causing a hubbub.)

INCY-WINCY

Usage example: *Incy-Wincy* spider climbed up the water spout. Down came the rain and washed the spider out. Out came the sun and dried up all the rain, so Incy-Wincy spider climbed up the spout again."

The words above are usually sung to, or by, children, and are sometimes accompanied by finger or hand movements. In some versions, Incy-Wincy is replaced by <u>*Itsy Bitsy*</u>. The song seems to have appeared in publication around 1910, but using "Blooming bloody" instead of Incy-Wincy. The more well-known variant started to appear from 1948 onwards. In addition to its use in the spider song, incy-wincy can be used to emphasize the diminutive nature of pretty much any small example of an object or creature. Often if the term is used, there is an added implication of cuteness associated with the item being described.

ITSY-BITSY

As mentioned above, *itsy-bitsy* sometimes appears as an alternative to *Incy-Wincy* in the song about the spider that climbed the water spout. This is because the two terms are pretty much synonymous. The itsy-bitsy variant is the one that forms the inspiration for the 2019 giant spider-themed horror movie *Itsy Bitsy* starring Bruce Davison, Denise Crosby, Eileen Dietz, and Matty Cardarople, directed by Micah Gallo.

In a less scary way, Itsy Bitsy is part of the main refrain from the novelty song "Itsy Bitsy Teenie Weenie Yellow Polkadot Bikini", written by Paul Vance and Lee Pockriss. It was released in June 1960 on a recording by Brian Hyland, with John Dixon conducting the orchestra. (Interestingly, on the B-side of the record was the song, "Don't *Dilly-Dally*, Sally".) The recording reached number one on the Billboard Hot 100. Various covers and versions have been recorded over the years, in assorted languages. A German version was titled, "Itsy Bitsy Teenie Weenie Honolulu-Strand-Bikini.

JELLY-BELLY

The *Jelly Belly* Candy Company is based in Fairfield, California, USA. It makes "Jelly Belly®" jelly beans as well as other candy. Previously the company was known by the names Herman Goelitz Candy Company and Goelitz Confectionery Company. In addition to the original location, candy is also manufactured in North Chicago, Illinois. A logistics and distribution center operates in Pleasant Prairie, Wisconsin. A manufacturing facility was opened in Rayong, Thailand in 2008.

JIBBER-JABBER

Probably derived from the word gibberish, *jibber-jabber* is rapid speech that a listener may find annoying or hard to understand. The expression is sometimes rendered as jibba-jabba. One very prominent individual known for using this expression is the actor, TV personality, and professional wrestler "Mr. T." (born Lawrence Tureaud) who played the characters B. A. Baracus in the 1980s television series, *The A-Team* and boxer Clubber Lang in the 1982 film, *Rocky III*.

Jibber Jabber is also the name of a Canadian children's television series. Jibba jabber was the name of a type of doll manufactured and sold by the company Ertl in the 1990s.

JIGGERY-POKERY

Jiggery pokery is a form of subterfuge or deceptive activity designed to manipulate or mislead people, or to confuse the facts of an issue. It implies somewhat more ill-intentioned motives than the similar activity of <u>*hocus-pocus*</u>. The term can also refer to manipulating or tinkering with the components of machinery, equipment or other systems to repair of restore functionality. "Getting the software to produce the reports in the new format took some considerable jiggery-pokery", one might say. In fact, the person writing this book actually made that statement during a meeting recently, unintentionally baffling a couple of people, much to his surprise and dismay.

Some people attribute the origin of the phrase to the nineteenth century Scots dialect expression, *joukery-pawkery*.

JINGLE-JANGLE

Jingle-jangle is the sound made by coins, keys or other metallic objects in a pocket, purse or container. Of course, <u>*bling-bling*</u> is likely to jingle-jangle when worn.

"Jingle Jangle" is the name a song released in 1968 performed by The Archies. The single reached number 10 on the Billboard Hot 100, and was also released as part of the 1969 album.

Jingle jangle is a fictional recreational drug featuring in the *Riverdale* television series, a teen drama based on characters appearing in the Archie Comics. The Archies song "Jingle Jangle" can be heard briefly during the Riverdale episode, "Chapter Thirty-Eight: As Above, So Below".

JINGLE MINGLE

I saw this one recently on a poster for an office Christmas party. The name *Jingle Mingle* was used for the event. Sadly, my schedule meant that I was not able to attend! Maybe next year.....

KILLER DILLER

If something is an outstanding, exceptional, astonishing, wonderful example of its category, it would be killer diller. "Jake bought a new car last week, a *killer diller* electric sports car", one might say of a friend's automotive purchase. Using just the word killer in a similar way works too, so the diller addition was undoubtedly added as reduplication.

The 1948 musical comedy movie *Killer Diller* featured performances by The Clark Brothers, Nat King Cole, Dusty Fletcher, Butterfly McQueen, Moms Mabley, the Four Congaroos and the Andy Kirk Orchestra. A later drama movie with the same title, *Killer Diller*, had a limited release in 2006, having been previously screened at the South by Southwest and Tribeca Film Festivals in 2004.

KITTY-CAT

Only marginally an example of reduplication, *kitty-cat* is an affectionate or childish term for a domestic cat (Felis sylvestris catus). The "kitty" component is a term in its own right for a young cat, kitten or kit. A similar term, pussy-cat, is slightly less frequently used, possibly because of one of the alternate meanings of the term pussy.

Returning to "kit", the term immediately, to me, brings to mind the riddle, "As I was going to St. Ives, I met a man with seven wives, Each wife had seven sacks, Each sack had seven cats, Each cat had seven kits: Kits, cats, sacks, and wives, How many were going to St. Ives?" Versions of the riddle appeared as early as the year 1730. (Spoiler alert!) There are at least six possible answers to the riddle: 2800, 2801, 2802, 1, "at least 1", and zero. The differences stem from an assessment as to exactly who is travelling to or from St. Ives (the narrator only, or all of the others as well), and whether the question is only asking about kits, cats, sacks and wives, thereby eliminating the narrator and the "man".

KNICK-KNACK

A knick-knack is a small ornament, or displayed keepsake or trinket that may adorn someone's home. The existence or presence of knick-knacks may reveal a questionable degree of taste on the part of the owner. Essentially, knick-knacks are individual items of *Bric-a-Brac*!

KAP CAP

For variety, I am including *Kap Cap* as an entry. This is an abbreviated name for the star Kappa Capricorni, which is visible to the naked eye in the constellation Capricornus. It has an apparent visual magnitude of 4.73. The star is situated at a distance from our Sun of about 294 light years.

LAFFY TAFFY

"Laffy Taffy®" is the name of the brand of taffy candies produced by the Ferrara Candy Company, a subsidiary of Ferrero. Each small candy is individually wrapped, and on the outside of each wrapper are printed silly jokes and riddles, mostly of the "dad joke" variety (although the jokes are often sent in by children). An example might be, "What's an owl's favorite subject? – Owlgebra." The candies themselves have bright colors and have artificial fruit flavors including strawberry, blueberry, watermelon, and blue raspberry

The brand has passed through multiple ownership. In the 1970s it was developed by Kathryn Beich Candies of Bloomington Illinois, then it was purchased by Nestlé in 1984, and then it was sold to Italian chocolatier Ferrero SpA, maker of "Nutella®", in 2018.

Laffy Taffy is also the title of a song by the hip-hop band D4L released in 2005. The lyrics include, "Girl, shake dat laffy taffy, That laffy taffy, Shake that laffy taffy, That laffy taffy, Girl, shake that laffy taffy, That laffy taffy......"

LATER-GATOR

This expression is a contraction of the departure salutation, "See you later, alligator!" The customary response to this full version would be, "In a while, crocodile!"

LEGAL BEAGLE

This term refers to an attorney or lawyer who has a reputation for being very determined, or who doggedly pursues the letter of the law. By extension, any person who strictly enforces rules, regulations and guidelines, regardless of whether or not they hold formal legal credentials, might be labelled a *legal beagle.*

LEGAL EAGLE

Any lawyer or attorney possessing greater skills than his or her peers, especially in terms of eloquence, creativity, or in-depth knowledge of legal matters and precedent, may be described as a *legal eagle*.

LOONEY TUNES

Looney Tunes is a multi-award winning American animated comedy series produced by Warner Bros. During its 1930 to 1969 period of production, the series introduced many famous and iconic cartoon characters including Bugs Bunny, Daffy Duck, Elmer Fudd, Porky Pig, Pepé Le Pew, Road Runner, Wile E. Coyote, Speedy Gonzales, Tasmanian Devil and many others. The long list of directors over the years included Tex Avery and Chuck Jones. Many of the characters at one time or another were voiced by voice actor Mel Blanc.

The name *Looney Tunes* is not really an example of true reduplication, but simply a rhyming combination. The name was inspired by Walt Disney's musical series *Silly Symphonies*, as was Warner Bros' own sister cartoon series *Merrie Melodies*.

Interestingly, in 2010, the name Looney Tunes was held up as an example of the newly-coined term "Mandela Effect", used to describe the phenomenon of shared false memories. Fiona Broome, a "paranormal consultant", started using the term Mandela Effect because of her own false memory of South African leader Nelson Mandela dying in the 1980s. Fiona claimed that this memory was shared by "perhaps thousands" of other people. Mandela in fact died in 2013. The idea of the Mandela Effect inspired a rash of theories as to its cause, including parallel universes and alternate reality timelines converging. So what has this to do with *Looney Tunes*? Well, a sizeable group of people claim that the name "was always" Looney <u>Toons,</u> and that somehow, sometime, it became

Looney Tunes in a mysterious way. One of the justifications is that, "Looney *Toons* makes more sense, because they are car*toons*". Such "reasoning" ignores the real origin and inspiration for the name *Looney Tunes*, as described in the previous paragraph above.

In my view, the deluded people just mentioned are actually experiencing something way more powerful than any Mandela Effect. They assume that the second word must be *Toons* because of the amazing power of reduplication. Believing that the word is *Toons* is actually a manifestation of a phenomenon which I am hereby dubbing with the term *Presumptive Reduplication*!

LOOSEY-GOOSEY

This term is used to describe an action or its result, or a situation or behaviour, which lacks quality or precision. The expression can be used in much the same way as the term *slap-dash* discussed later in this book. Another meaning of loosey-goosey is that something or someone is excessively relaxed, the opposite of uptight or taut. Muscles can be all loosey-goosey, for example, after vigorous, tiring, exercise.

LOVEY-DOVEY

People are acting in a lovey-dovey way if they are displaying romantic affection in a visible or detectable way. Actions, text messages, email and discussions can all exhibit lovey-dovey characteristics.

In his 1977 version of the song, "One bourbon, one scotch, one beer", George Thorogood describes his landlady as having been "lovey dovey" for five years, right up to the day that he could not pay his rent on time. At that point, the landlady, "Ain't got nothing nice to say". After George subsequently claims to have found a job and says that he can indeed pay his rent, the landlady is briefly lovey-dovey once more. George then packs up his things and slips out the back door, eventually ending up in a bar. What a story!

LOW BLOW

In the sport of boxing, regulations state that punches may not be inflicted below waist level. *Low blows* are prohibited! In broader parlance, a low blow is a general term for any attack which is, or is perceived to be, unsportsmanlike, unfair, unjust, unscrupulous, unwarranted, or unprincipled. Such an attack could be physical, but it is more likely to be a verbal attack, a legal maneuver, or other underhand action. Typically a verbal low blow would also be a poor quality remark, or one that lacks direct relevance to the matter at hand. "While we were arguing about who should cook supper, my spouse brought up the time that that I got drunk in the pub after work and missed the last train home. That was a real low blow!"

MAYBE BABY

Often used simply as a way to turn the plain old word maybe into a more folksy reduplicated delight, Maybe Baby is also the name of a song recorded by Buddy Holly and the Crickets in 1957. Almost certainly, the song brought the term *maybe baby* into common use. The song has been covered by many prominent performers. *Maybe Baby* is also the name of a British movie written and directed by Ben Elton, starring Hugh Laurie and Joely Richardson, released in the year 2000.

In a more literal sense, maybe baby is used by some potential adoptive parents when referring to a specific child that they hope will become part of their family. "Our maybe baby is a beautiful child called Meghan", they might say. "Maybe Baby®" is also the name of a fertility ovulation testing device marketed by Care Pharmaceuticals.

In a more street slang context, maybe baby might be used to describe a woman that someone hopes (possibly in their wildest dreams) might someday be their partner or date. "You know that Miranda in finance? She's my maybe baby!"

MATCHY-MATCHY

Matchy-matchy is a term used in the fashion industry to describe someone or something that is coordinated to an excessive degree, using too many of the same colors, patterns, types of fabrics, or styles of accessories. Being first added as a term to the *Oxford Dictionary of English* in 2010, it remains a matter of opinion and debate as to whether being matchy-matchy represents good or bad taste. As the lead character points out in the 2009 movie, "Bruno", military camouflage uniforms ("outfits") are too matchy-matchy!

MISH-MASH

The term *mish-mash* may be used for any item or concept which consists of components or other subsidiary items or concepts amassed from other sources. One could claim, for example, that the plot of a movie was a mish-mash of themes from other movies. Superficially this term is similar to *hodge-podge*, but tends to refer to non-physical creations, and does not necessarily imply that the components of the whole are mismatched.

MOD-PLOD

In the United Kingdom, there exists a civilian special police force within the Ministry of Defence (MOD), called the Ministry of Defence Police (MDP). The force is separate from the Royal Military Police and other Service Police organizations. Its role is to provide armed security and counter terrorism protection, as well as to provide uniformed policing and some investigative services, to Ministry of Defence property, personnel, and installations throughout the United Kingdom. In practice, this usually means that most military personnel encounter MDP staff in circumstances where they would rather not! They may be denied entry to an establishment because of incorrect credentials. They may fall foul of the law and get investigated. As a result the MDP, although a vital component of the MOD, tends to be viewed in a less than favorable light by some members of the military. Accordingly, the military resorts to the time-honoured tradition of assigning a disparaging nickname. Members of the MDP are customarily referred to as *MOD-PLOD*s. The "MOD" portion of the name is a verbalization of the standard abbreviation for the Ministry of Defence. The "PLOD" part comes from another, more widespread within the UK, term for a police officer generally, i.e. "Plod", or even "Police Constable (PC) Plod". This derives from the name of the Policeman character in the "Noddy" series of children's books by Enid Blyton, "Mister Plod", which in turn is an allusion to the stereotype of the friendly but authoritative police officer walking (plodding) his patrol area (his "beat"). Phew!

MOO THRU

A rural ice cream store, *Moo Thru* was founded by fourth generation dairy farmer Ken Smith. The Smith Family has owned and operated a dairy farm in Fauquier County, Virginia, USA for decades. With the help of his family, Ken opened Moo Thru in June 2010. The company has been growing ever since and now includes several additional franchised locations. The family farm, where the herd of champion Holstein cows are fed the healthiest possible diet, is located just two miles away from the original ice cream store. The ice cream is handcrafted and slow churned in Remington, Virginia. Each flavoring ingredient is hand-selected, fresh, and locally-sourced whenever possible.

MOP-TOP

A *mop-top* is a disparaging term for a largish shock of head hair, styled to accentuate volume rather than length. The wearer of such fashionable hirsuteness thus resembles that wonderful device used to swab floors, the humble domestic mop.

MOSS BROS

Moss Brothers is a menswear specialist firm of tailors founded in Covent Garden, London, in 1851. Still going strong as the Moss Bros Group PLC, the company continues to provide formal and casual articles of clothing to discerning gentlemen worldwide. Even before the name of the company was modified to include "Bros" as the abbreviation for Brothers, most people called the organization Moss Bros anyway. My own Royal Air Force No. 1 and No. 5 uniforms were tailored by Moss Bros when I purchased them in 1980.

MUMBO-JUMBO

Along with jibber-jabber, this expression is part of the title of this handy-dandy guide. So, what does it mean? Well, that's an appropriate question to ask, I suppose, about a term that describes words and language that don't have meaning to a person hearing them. The phrase is used to describe meaningless or confusing speech or writing, as well as any associated actions and rituals, often in a derogatory way. Specific terminology used by certain professions, such as business managers, IT practitioners or scientists, may be called *mumbo-jumbo* by people who are not part of those groups. In turn, those indulging in mumbo-jumbo often do so in a cliquish, exclusionary way.

Mumbo Jumbo was derived from a West African Mandinka word *Maamajomboo*, used to describe a masked ceremonial dancer who took part in certain religious ceremonies. The explorer and writer Mungo Park in his 1795 book "Travels in the Interior of Africa" mentioned "Mumbo Jumbo", a character that Mandinka men would dress up as when it was necessary to resolve domestic disputes, especially arguments amongst wives involved in polygamous marriage with the said husband. In the event that you decide to research this ritual in more detail yourself, you will probably quickly agree with me that it was essentially an example of public spousal humiliation and physical abuse.

NAMBY-PAMBY

Many web searches for the word, "reduplication" will return results that explain the linguistic concept and then offer up *namby-pamby* as a classic example. I am not sure why this should be the case, but it is indeed a good example. Common meanings of the term namby-pamby, when used as an adjective, include weak, indecisive, lacking substance or character, insipid, or feeble in behaviour. (An occasional variant of this term is mamby-pamby.)

NATER-TATER

Those fortunate enough to be named Nathaniel often have to hear their name abbreviated in various ways. Nathan is a common shortened version of the name, and Nate is a frequent familiar abbreviation. Sometimes, as with any name, a shortened version is then re-lengthened to differ from the original to become a nickname. "Nater" is not uncommon as a friendly name for Nathaniel, and *Nater-Tater* is a further lengthening. This last version, of course, has a humorous allusion to that wonderful tuber, the potato, with in some areas is referred to as a tater.

When our son Nater Tater was about 14, we came up with a more imposing variant of his name, to add some additional panache, so that he could be proud in social gatherings. Basically, we Frenchified his name (no, not French-fried), by awarding him the title, *"Nathaniel de la Pomme-de-Terre"*.

NECK-UP CHECK-UP

A psychiatric evaluation or other diagnostic procedure. Most often, this term would be used pejoratively, for example, "Anyone turning down an offer of free pizza needs a *neck-up check-up!*"

NIFTY FIFTY

Widely used in names of businesses and products, Nifty Fifty and variants of it have some specific well established current and older uses as well. In photography, a 50 mm lens fitted as standard to most SLR film cameras was sometimes called a nifty fifty. The Nifty Fifty was a term used in the mid-1900s to refer to the top fifty "blue chip" stocks. The Nifty 50 is an Indian stock market index. In the 1980s, Honda produced a motor scooter with a 49 cc engine capacity called the Honda Eve or Honda Spree or Nifty 50 (NQ50). Nifty Fifty's® is the name of a chain of 1950s diner-themed restaurants operating in Pennsylvania and New Jersey in the USA.

NIGGLYWIGGLY

This term is widely claimed to be the official name for the piece of paper that protrudes from the foil at the top of each piece of Hershey's® Kisses® candy. When asked directly in March 2013 via the corporate Facebook page whether the name for these paper strips was indeed, *NigglyWiggly*, Hershey's responded as follows: "The little flags of paper placed in the foil of our HERSHEY'S KISSES Candies are known as *plumes*. They allow our fans to know which sweet indulgence they'll be consuming, as the flavor of candy is printed on the plume. Hope this clears up the confusion!"

NIGHT FLIGHT

Night Flight is a 1931 novel, published in French as *Vol de Nuit*. The author was French writer and pilot Antoine de

Saint-Exupéry. The novel has been published in multiple languages, and is an international bestseller. A movie inspired by the novel was released in 1933.

The main theme of the novel was the concept of sacrificing personal considerations for a greater cause. The characters were all associated with air mail deliveries during the early years of commercial aviation. Rivière is the station chief of an Argentinian airline that is the first to use night flights as a way of getting the mail through ahead of the competition. The story addresses the last hours of a pilot, Fabien, whose aircraft is making the perilous Patagonia run. Fabien's plane gets caught in a vicious storm, runs out of fuel, and is lost. All the while, Fabien's wife is waiting anxiously, but in vain, for his return. The novel gained additional popularity during the World's major conflicts of the 1930s and 1940s as a result of its theme of self-sacrifice for the greater good.

Various products have been inspired by the events of the novel, including the perfume *Vol de Nuit*, by Guerlain.

Antoine de Saint-Exupéry was himself an aviator. While flying with the Free French Air Force, he undertook a mission in an unarmed P-38 aircraft on July 31, 1944. Departing from Corsica, his assigned goal was to gather intelligence on German troop movements in and around the Rhone Valley preceding "Operation Dragoon", the planned invasion of southern France by Allied forces. Antoine de Saint-Exupéry did not return from the mission.

NIGHT FRIGHT

Night Fright was a 1967 American science-fiction horror film starring John Agar, directed by James A. Sullivan. In the UK, for whatever odd reason, the title for VHS video release was, *E.T.N.: The Extraterrestrial Nasty*. The plot revolves around mysterious killings of the students from the local college. It transpires that the "murderer" is actually a mutated alligator,

transformed into a bullet-proof marauder by a NASA cosmic
ray experiment.

Sometimes *night fright* is used as a term to describe troubling,
often recurring, nightmares that cause someone to shout or
move violently in their sleep. These are a more severe form of
the far more common "hypnic jerk" reflex. It is not unusual
for someone, just as he or she is falling off to sleep, to get a
sudden flash-like dream where they feel that they are falling or
tripping, and as a result startle themselves awake. The reason
for these hypnic jerks being so common is a matter of debate.
One theory is that they represent some form of survival
instinct or genetic memory from the tree-dwelling primate
stage of human evolution, when falling asleep and falling out
of a tree would likely spell disaster. Much as I enjoyed
climbing trees as a child, I personally do not attach much
credence to this demeaning theory.

NIP-SLIP

Is voyeurism a universal human affliction? Perhaps.
Certainly, the popular media, at least the less high-brow
components, do seem obsessed with sating a perceived
appetite for voyeurism among the world's population. The
assumption is that the viewership or readership of their
publications wants nothing more than to see pictures of
famous people accidentally revealing more of their skin to
view than is apparently intended. Movie personalities,
politicians, members of royalty and others all risk having any
accidentally exposed "private" area of their bodies
immediately becoming very public via professional, amateur
and social media. An inadvertently revealed nipple, buttock or
pubic region could "go viral" or be transformed into a meme in
a matter of seconds. Paparazzi photographers are constantly
on the lookout for "wardrobe malfunctions", whether they be
intentional or accidental, that can captured for all to view.
One target of such shutter-bugs is a *nip-slip*, whereby a female
celebrity unintentionally displays a nipple to the watching

world. Any picture taken at the exact moment of such a prurient glimpse will be promptly broadcast for the mass titillation of the viewing public.

NITTY-GRITTY

Some people in this world are content to have topics, concepts and knowledge presented to them at a summarized, overview level. Others prefer to be given the full details of whatever component of the knowledge is of specific relevance to them. This latter group prefers to, "get down to the *nitty-gritty*".

NOTABLE QUOTABLE

A term that came to be fairly common around 2020, *notable quotable* (sometimes hyphenated) is used by many news shows, blogs and other news media. Typically the term serves as a title for a news segment that discusses newsworthy quotes or statements from politicians, celebrities, or other prominent individuals or organizations. Various products and merchandise that include the words "notable quotable" as part of their names are available, such as wall calendars and wallet cards. These items feature quotations from significant or inspirational people.

NO-TELL MOTEL

An establishment where people rent bedrooms so that liaisons that they want to be kept secret can be conducted privately, may be referred to as a *no-tell motel*. Such a motel might well charge by the hour, rather than per night. There might also be an extra charge for sheets! Discretion is normally guaranteed. Paying with cash, rather than by credit card where a charge would appear on a statement to be found by a spouse or partner, is perfectly acceptable. Motels that have a reputation for such business are probably best avoided if someone actually wants to sleep. The constant coming and going of

occupants of other rooms, and the noisy banging (of doors),
are not conducive to a good night's rest.

NO-SHOW

When summarizing attendance numbers at an event or
gathering, someone might specifically state the number of *no-
shows*. The term relates to individuals who had signed up or
registered for the event, but who did not in the end actually
show up. Tracking no-shows can be helpful for future
planning of similar events. When costly arrangements are
being made for catering, event facilities, and other necessities,
having some feel for what percentage of registered attendees
are likely to actually arrive in person can be helpful, and can
save unnecessary expenditures by an event organizer.

The airline industry in the United States and several other
countries has a practice of deliberately over-selling seats on
domestic and international aircraft flights, on the assumption
that somewhere between 5 and 15 percent of booked
passengers will end up being no-shows. This assumption is
based on previous records of ratios of actual passenger
numbers compared to booked passengers. Various adjusting
algorithms are applied to reflect specific routes, times of year,
and other variables. Despite this precision, it is not
uncommon for no-show numbers to end up being lower than
predicted for a specific flight, with more passengers arriving
and wanting seats than actually exist in the aircraft. In such
an event, announcements start to be made at the gate area
offering all sorts of inducements, often in the form of vouchers
for future travel, to any passengers willing to surrender their
bookings and to be moved to an alternate flight. If these
inducements do not resolve the over-booking problem,
passengers may simply be "bumped" to an alternate flight
against their wishes.

ODD-BOD

A slightly dated way of referring to an anonymous person in the United Kingdom was to say, "bod". For example, one might say that, "Two bods walked into the pub last night and beat everyone at darts". Another might say, "That new bod at work got fired after just two days!" The derivation is almost certainly from an abbreviation of "body".

In a situation where someone is considered by others to be somewhat peculiar in character or behaviour, the person might be labelled, "a bit of an *odd-bod*". Although bod and odd-bod are essentially gender-neutral terms, they are more commonly used when referring to male persons.

ODDLE-PODDLE

One of my absolute favorite children's television shows was *Watch with Mother,* broadcast by the BBC between 1953 and 1973. Most of all, I enjoyed the characters Bill and Ben (the Flowerpot Men), who were stringed puppet figures made of flowerpots. They dwelt and played at the bottom of a suburban garden amongst the tools and equipment used by the "man who worked in the garden". While the man was away at lunch (he was never seen by the viewers), Bill and Ben would wake up and emerge from two large flowerpots in which they slept between adventures. On emerging, they would greet their friend, a flower called Little Weed, using a strange language that followed the tones of expressive English, but which mainly used childlike sounds instead of words. The language was called, *Oddle Poddle* by its inventor, Peter Hawkins. Bill and Ben always conversed in Oddle Poddle, and at the end of each episode would say goodbye to Little Weed in Oddle Poddle by saying, ""Babap ickle Weed!". At the time there were those who claimed that exposing children to Oddle Poddle would hinder their development and their learning of correct English. Similar ridiculous claims were made regarding *Teletubby* speak some twenty years later.

OKEY-DOKEY

Okey-dokey is, of course, simply a folksy way of saying, "OK". So the underlying questions are what does OK (or okay) mean, and where did the term OK come from?

OK, let's address those questions. Actually, that previous sentence indicates one use of the term OK, namely as a way of indicating that something – a discussion, meeting, event or course of action – is now getting started or is underway. The more common usage, though, is to indicate assent or agreement to something. The term can also be used to indicate that the condition of something is reasonable, as opposed to exceptional or poor. Someone's health could be OK, as opposed to great, for example.

With regard to theories for origin of the term, three main contenders are prominent. One is that the origin is from the Native American Choctaw language. In 1825, Christian missionaries Cyrus Byington and Alfred Wright translated the Bible into the Choctaw language, and ended many sentences with "okeh", meaning "it is so".

A second proposed origin is that OK arose during something called the Boston Abbreviation Fad, which began in 1838. Somewhat humorous expressions became common such as OFM, "our first men," to refer the US Founding Fathers, NG to mean, "no go," GT for "gone to Texas," and SP, for "small potatoes." One predecessor of OK was OW, "oll wright". OK seems to have been an intentional humorous misspelling of "all correct" from "Oll Korrect".

A third possible etymology is that the term, "Kay" came to the United States via a West African language, possibly Mande or Bantu.

OKEY-COKEY (DIDDLY-DOKEY),

This term, either just as *okey-cokey* or in the full version *okey-cokey diddly-dokey*, is again an elaboration of the simple, "OK". As such, it is an even folksier version of the term okey-dokey discussed in the previous entry. All of this just goes to show how much the human brain loves the concept of linguistic reduplication!

OOEY-GOOEY

If something is sticky, it might reasonable be said to be gooey. If something is particularly sticky, then it might be referred to as being *ooey-gooey*. One of the most frequent encounters with gooeyness that people experience is with sweet cakes, deserts or candy. Gooey or ooey-gooey butter cake, a traditional cake resembling a brownie in consistency, originated in St. Louis, Missouri. It is fairly dense, made with flour, sugar, eggs and butter, and is usually dusted with powdered sugar.

This association with sweetness gives rise to the other common meaning of the phrases ooey and ooey-gooey, namely the characteristic of being overly sentimental or affectionate, or behaving in that manner.

PEE-PEE

Pee is a euphemistic word for urine (when used as a noun) or to urinate (when used as a verb). It derives from the initial letter of a more vulgar word with the same said meanings. The reduplication into *pee-pee* is a childish variant. Sometimes, pee-pee is also used as reference to the organ or area of the body involved in the process of urination. The term "pee-pee head" is therefore a way to call someone a dick-head!

PEE-WEE

If something is *pee-wee*, it is a small or diminutive example of its class. A person, creature of other object can possess pee-wee characteristics. In the United States, pee-wee is also an age-specific level of youth sports. Children may participate in pee-wee baseball, football or soccer leagues.

For many people, the words pee-wee immediately bring to mind Pee-wee Herman, a character created by comedian Paul Reubens. Pee-wee Herman featured in television series and movies in the 1980s. The movies were the 1985 *Pee-wee's Big Adventure* and the *1988 Big Top Pee-wee*. In 1991 Paul Reubens was arrested for indecent exposure in an adult theater. The incident was widely publicized. After a number of years in relative obscurity, Reubens gradually returned to the role of Pee-wee Herman, and in 2016 the Netflix movie *Pee-wee's Big Holiday* was released.

PETER METER

A fictitious measuring instrument used to evaluate the length and/or angular relationship to the ground of a male reproductive organ (Peter). Of course, this is a tongue-in-cheek term. A more generic angle-measuring instrument used by doctors to determine, for example, the extent to which an elbow of a patient can be bent, is known as goniometer. Note that the root word for the first component of "goniometer" is entirely different from that for the first part of the word "gonad".

PIGGLY-WIGGLY

Piggly-Wiggly is the name of a chain of excellent grocery stores from the Southern states of the USA. Many people from outside the region may recall the name being used in the movie, "Driving Miss Daisy".

If you can only visit one Piggly-Wiggly in your lifetime, make it the Bigley Piggly-Wiggly located in Bigley, West Virginia!

PITTER-PATTER

It is very hard to utter the words *pitter-patter* without thinking about tiny feet. The most frequent usage of the term pitter-patter is associated with a realization that someone may have become pregnant recently, but has yet to announce the fact. A discerning friend might react to an inadvertent letting-slip of the condition by saying, "Do I hear the patter of tiny feet in the near future?"

Of course, other usages for the term do exist, but as with the previous example they tend to be onomatopoeic. Raindrops, for example, can pitter-patter on tree leaves during a gentle shower.

POCKET ROCKET

This term, as with many in this book, is used in different ways with different meanings. I am a motorcyclist. Motorcycles come in many different types and styles, such as cruisers, tourers, streetfighters and sportbikes. The last of these categories, sportbikes, are the fast "crotch-rockets" that may pass you on the road at a great rate of speed. Typically they have fairings and low bars, and resemble racing motorcycles that are more normally seen on closed racing circuits. A few years ago a flood of miniaturized motorcycles became available for use on private property. When riding on one, a person would have an appearance somewhat resembling that of a clown at a circus riding a tiny bicycle. Anyway, the sportbike mini-replicas could still achieve a speed of around 40 mph, and so earned the name *pocket rocket*.

One alternate use of the term pocket rocket is as a humorous description of a small "personal massager" device, which applies buzzing vibrations to parts of the body at the discretion of the owner. I consider it unlikely that such an artifact would be carried around in someone's pocket very often. As an addition to an overnight bag for a short stay in a hotel or _no-tell motel_, however, these devices are likely more of a mainstay.

POOPER-SCOOPER

Most pet dogs lead a pretty happy and contented life. They have loving owners, their health is monitored and maintained through exercise and visits to the vet, and they are fed nutritious food in ample quantities. Because pet dogs are so abundant, in many regions and localities pet owners are encouraged by social pressure, or required by legal ordinance, to pick up and dispose of their pets' fecal deposits. Various techniques exist for carrying out this task. Possibly the most common is to put one's hand into a plastic bag, grab the odorous nugget, deftly invert the bag around it, and tie-off the top of the bag ready for disposal in a waste receptacle. For those repelled by the squidgy feel of the warm mass through the bag, various tools and grabbers might be used to lift the poop into the bag. Generically, such devices are called _pooper-scooper_s.

POTATO-POTATO

This term describes the sound made by a large-capacity, air-cooled, V-twin motorcycle engine when it is idling. When a motorcycle with such an engine (a Harley Davidson, for example) is sitting beside you in a line of traffic waiting at a stop light, the sound you hear will be _potato-potato_. Once the light changes and the traffic moves off, the motorcycle engine noise will change to a satisfying roar.

POW-WOW

Commonly used as a term for a discussion involving relevant and carefully-selected participants, a _pow-wow_ more accurately is a Native American term for a social gathering, usually involving singing, dancing and traditional cultural activities. The words originate from the Narragansett word "powwaw", meaning spiritual leader. Many different Native American tribes and communities continue to hold pow-wows.

RAG-TAG

Most commonly followed by the words, "army" or, "group", *rag-tag* refers to an assemblage of individuals who are loosely organized or controlled. There is also an implication that such people would be unkempt and probably not uniform in appearance, aside from their shared scruffiness. As an example, a corporation's computer security might be breached by a rag-tag group of hackers. Invading forces might be repelled by a rag-tag group of mercenaries and militia members.

The origin of the term dates to around the sixteenth century. Everyday members of the public, the *hoi-polloi*, might be condescendingly described as tag-rag by those considering themselves superior to them. Gradually the tem became rag, tag and bobtail, which in addition to the meaning just stated, could also mean an entire group of people, both skilled and unskilled. More recently, the bobtail component was dropped, leaving just rag-tag.

The UK children's television series, *Watch with Mother* that I have mentioned elsewhere, included appearances by Rag, Tag and Bobtail on the Thursday slot from around 1953 to 1965. Three puppet characters were featured in various short stories: Rag, a hedgehog; Tag, a mouse; and Bobtail, a rabbit. My two older sisters and I once owned three pet rabbits when we were growing up. We named them Rag, Tag and Bobtail.

RANG-TANG

When I have heard this term used, it has related mainly to a situation whereby one or more people are *rang-tang*ing around. Such behaviour would involve acting in an excited but haphazard fashion, probably with much noise and unproductive dashing around.

In the early twentieth century, the term Rang Tang was used as a slang term for orangutan. A 1927 Broadway musical, *Rang Tang*, used that slang term as inspiration. The production was very successful. The plot revolved around a series of comedy misadventures that befall a pair of barbers who steal an aircraft, then crash in Africa and have to deal with fierce animals and hostile inhabitants of deserts and jungles.

RAZZLE-DAZZLE

The expression *razzle-dazzle* dates from at least 1885. When used, it refers to a confusing, colorful, noisy, raucous display, designed to attract (or as a sports move to distract) attention. The term derived as a back-reduplication of the more straightforward word dazzle. The expression has appeared extensively in various guises in popular culture. "Razzle Dazzle" is a song from the 1975 musical *Chicago*. Deep Purple also release a song called "Razzle Dazzle" on the album *Bananas*. Buck-Tick released an album in 2010 called *Razzle Dazzle*. A BBC children's TV series was called *Razzle Dazzle*. Other examples are plentiful!

In 1981 the movie *Stripes* was released, starring Bill Murray, Harold Ramis, Warren Oates, P. J. Soles, Sean Young, and John Candy, about a group of semi-willing Army recruits. In the movie, as part of the recruit graduation parade, Bill Murray leads his platoon in a very unconventional drill routine, including a series of moves called for by his command, "Razzle---Dazzle!" While many people will state

that the movie was the origin for the Razzle Dazzle drill
routine, I know from a first-hand account that it was
commonly performed by, and popular with, recruits during
United States Air Force basic training at Lackland AFB in
Texas five years earlier in 1977. Variations on the Razzle
Dazzle routine now form part of many official drill displays in
the USA.

RIFF-RAFF

It has surprised me, while compiling reduplicated phrases, to
find just how many seem to be associated with derogatory
ways of describing people considered to be of lower social
standing than the speaker or writer using the phrase. *Riff raff*
is an example of this sad phenomenon. The term means
disreputable people, the rabble, or the great unwashed. One
commonly-suggested etymology is that the term came from
Middle English, where *ryffe raffe* meant every sinle one, from
rif and *raf*, in turn deriving from the French *rif e raf* meaning
altogether.

Riff Raff, often written RiFF RAFF, is the stage name of Horst
Christian Simco, an American rap artist from Houston, Texas.

RIGHTY-TIGHTY

One memory aid for knowing which way to turn a bolt to
tighten it, and which way to turn it to loosen it, is the phrase
"righty-tighty, lefty-loosey." This is helpful unless one thinks
a little more deeply. Do you turn to top of the bolt cap towards
the right, or turn the bottom of the bolt cap to the right? Well,
I suppose you could assume that righty-tighty means using the
right hand and turning the bolt from the right side towards the
body, whereas lefty-loosey would be using the left hand and
turning the left side of the bot inwards towards the body. But
hey, what if the bolt has a left-hand thread? What if the bolt
head is facing away from you? Just forget the memory aid
phrase, and rely on muscle memory!

RINKTUM-INKTUM

"Rinktum Inktum" is the title of a rather odd song with unsettling lyrics recorded by Red Foley and Lulu Belle in 1934, and released as a B-side to "Going Out West This Fall". Both songs were written by John Lair. The unsettling component is the stated age of the amorous character voiced by Lulu Belle, namely 16 years. This troubling aspect is worse still in the version of the song printed in the 1937 edition of the *Alka-Seltzer Song Book* (yes, such a thing existed) where her age is 15 years.

RINKY-DINK

Something that is of inferior quality of its type, or that is outdated, amateurish, backward or small-time, might be referred to as *rinky-dink*. "Which airline are you flying with on your trip?" a friend might ask. "Well, not one of the major carriers, just a rinky-dink regional outfit", one might respond.

Separately, I have heard the term used as a way to indicate that someone is not engaged in any specific or important activity, but simply passing time or attending to minor chores. When a family member phones you and says, "Hope I'm not catching you at a busy time!" you might reply, "No it's OK, I'm just rinky-dinking".

RIP-RAP

Rip-rap is rubble, chunks of stone or other strong protective material placed along shorelines, around bridge piers, and in other locations that might otherwise be eroded by the action of waves, tides, flowing ice and boat wakes. The term may originate from the nautical "rip" meaning an area of rough water, often in a shallow area or close to shore, and "rap" meaning to knock against something. Placing and maintaining rip-rap is an expensive undertaking, but the possible consequential costs of dealing with or repairing erosion would likely be considerably higher.

RISSELDY-ROSSELDY

In the 1963 Alfred Hitchcock movie *The Birds*, the song the children are singing in the school as the crows mass outside is known as "Risseldy-Rosseldy", an Americanized variation of the Scottish folk song "Wee Cooper O' Fife". Hitchcock cleverly uses the ominous chanting of the song to build tension and to create an oppressive atmosphere.

The lyrics of the original folklore song contain troubling themes of domestic abuse. The American version as used in the film omits these themes. Most versions of the song contain additional nonsense reduplications such as nickety nackety and willickey wallackey.

ROACH COACH

At the time or writing, Food Trucks have become very popular in districts where people venture out of offices and places of work to buy lunch. The trucks are a common site in designated areas in most city centers or down-town areas. Many different cuisines are available, all freshly-prepared, delicious and satisfying. Food truck aficionados enthusiastically monitor various mobile Apps to find locations of trucks and the offerings available.

All of the above is a far cry from the earlier version of a food truck that many factory workers and members of the military on bases and posts around the world might recall. Small vans carrying very basic snack foods (including *Ding Dongs* and *Ho Hos* of course), candy, potato chips, simple sandwiches, pies, plus soda, hot tea or coffee, would stop at various units, aircraft hangars and work sites at scheduled times. Workers would then take a short break to avail themselves of the delights of the *roach coach*, as such vans were often called, semi-jokingly. In the UK, a van of this type in the military would normally be run by the NAAFI (Navy, Army and Air Forces Institute), and would be called the "NAAFI Wagon".

On some bases, for workers who can get away from their main location for lunch, various canteens and simple cafeterias, essentially non-mobile versions of roach coaches, might be available. Disdainful appellations for these establishments might include, "The Greasy Spoon", "The Scarf and Barf", and "The Choke and Puke".

ROGER-DODGER

Saying, "Roger" is the traditional method in the military, during radio or other voice-only communication, to indicate that a message is acknowledged and understood. But why Roger? Why not "Susan" or "Peter"? The explanation is simple in that Roger was a way of say the letter, "R", meaning that the message was "**r**eceived and understood". If you are thinking that it should be Romeo rather than Roger , that's because you have in mind the current phonetic alphabet, the one that goes, Alpha, Bravo, Charlie.......through to Romeo. The earlier phonetic alphabet, from the World War II era, went, Able, Baker, Charlie........through to Roger.

So, what about the "dodger" part of *roger-dodger*? This is simply a way of reducing the formality of the phrase when using it in every day conversation, and adding a light-hearted component.

Some folks might say that "10-4" is the military response meaning "yes". This is not quite correct. "10-4" is one of the "10 Codes", or ten signals, which are brevity codes used to represent common phrases. Law enforcement agencies make the greatest use of 10 Codes, and previously users of Citizens Band (CB) radio would use the codes extensively, almost as a way to show that they belonged to the CB radio fraternity. The police version of ten-codes is officially known as the APCO

Project 14 Aural Brevity Code, developed during 1937–1940 and expanded in 1974 by the Association of Public-Safety Communications Officials-International (APCO). However, the lack of absolute standardization of some of the code meanings between different agencies led to the U.S. federal government recommending, in 2006, that they be discontinued, and that plain language should be used in preference.

ROLY-POLY

Anything that is *roly-poly* is likely to have a rotund or rounded appearance, possible by design or nature, or perhaps as a result of neglect or overindulgence. In Britain, a sweet desert called roly-poly is made using thick pastry, spread thickly with sweet jam, and rolled up and cooked in the oven. Usually server hot with warm vanilla-based custard, roly-poly can lead to a state of roly-polyness when consumed in excessive quantities.

As a child in England, I used to call woodlice "roly-polies". These delightful creatures would scuttle around on walls and in the grass. When touched, they would roll up like miniature armadillos and could be carried around in my pockets, to the long-suffering, good-natured frustration of my sweet mother. When I first met my future wife in the United States, it was a delight to find out that she, as a child, had shared my fascination with woodlice, also calling them roly-polies and also carrying them around as cute little pets.

ROOTY-TOOT (-TOOT)

An animated short comedy film released by Columbia Pictures in 1951, *Rooty Toot Toot* was nominated for an Academy Award for Best Animated Short Film in 1951. It lost out to the Tom and Jerry cartoon, *The Two Mouseketeers*.

The studio album *The Lonesome Jubilee* released by John Cougar Mellencamp in 1987 contained the song "Rooty Toot Toot". A single of the song was released the following year.

The Christmas song "Santa Claus Is Comin' to Town" by J. Fred Coots and Haven Gillespie, first sung on Eddie Cantor's radio show in November 1934, includes as part of the lyrics, "With little tin horns, little toy drums; Rooty toot toots and rummy tum tums; Santa Claus is coming to town"

The shorter phrase *rooty-toot* is an onomatopoeic term for something that is lively or noisy, and specifically can refer to an early style of jazz music (based on the extensive use of trumpets in the genre).

Rooty-toot can also be used as an interjection of pleasant surprise when something good or exciting is happening or is planned. As with any such expression indicating that something is exceptional, rooty-toot can be also used sarcastically, often receded by the word *well*. "So we are going to spend our vacation clearing out the garage. Well rooty-toot!"

ROOTY-TOOTY

Anything that can be described as *rooty-tooty* will probably be in possession of *rooty-toot* or *rooty-toot-toot* characteristics or qualities.

A signature pancake offering at the IHOP® restaurant chain in the USA is the menu item, "Rooty Tooty Fresh 'N Fruity®" Pancakes. This delicious offering consists of four thick buttermilk pancakes, served with fruit and finished with fluffy whipped topping.

RUMBLE-TUMBLE

Most typically, *rumble-tumble* is used in a similar way to the term rough and tumble, describing a chaotic, possibly confrontational, <u>*hurly-burly*</u> type of activity.

A historical use was for the name of an attachment at the back of a horse-drawn carriage, added or folded into place as needed to provide additional seating (often to be occupied by servants) or to provide storage for luggage. The derived term rumble-seat remains in fairly frequent use today to refer to additional seating in a car or van that can be folded up and put into use when required. The rumble part of the term comes from the fact that such seats, unlike the main passenger seating area, were not positioned mid-way between the suspension springs. Road vibration and swaying from ruts and bumps were therefore much more noticeable, making the ride rather uncomfortable.

RUMPY-PUMPY

This is a visually-descriptive way of referring to sexual intercourse. Typically the activity so described would be of a casual, illicit or vigorous nature. In some ways it could be said that *rumpy-pumpy* is the act that consummates instances of <u>*hanky-panky*</u> that probably led up to it. Rumpy-pumpy appears to be a relatively recent term, possibly first appearing in the 1950s in Scotland.

RUB-A-DUB

Meaning "Pub" (public house or bar), this is an example of Cockney Rhyming Slang, possibly inspired by the nursery rhyme discussed in the next entry.

RUB-A-DUB DUB

"Rub-a-Dub Dub" is a nursery rhyme known to many people. The most common version goes as follows: "Rub-a-dub-dub, Three men in a tub, And who do you think they be? The butcher, the baker, the candlestick maker, And all of them out to sea."

Many nursery rhymes have an underlying background whereby the origin stems from social or political commentary, often in a veiled way. "Rub-a-dub dub" is no exception. Dating possibly as far back as the fourteenth century, early versions referred to three *maids* in a tub. Probably, this alluded to an early version of a peep show found at fairs and carnivals know as a "tub", wherein sat maidens in various stages of undress, viewed by lascivious lechers through holes in the tub walls. Early versions of the rhyme, as per the following example, highlighted the hypocrisy of some otherwise respectable local businessmen: "Hey! rub-a-dub, ho! rub-a-dub, three maids in a tub, And who do you think were there? The butcher, the baker, the candlestick-maker, And all of them gone to the fair.

SACKY-LACKY

This is an affectionate term used by some residents of the Carolinas in the USA to refer to the State of South Carolina. As mentioned earlier in this volume, the equivalent appellation for North Carolina is *Cacky-Lacky*.

SAT NAV

Sat nav is an abbreviation of "satellite navigation", and is most commonly used in British English to refer to the receiving and display system for navigational data installed in cars and other vehicles. In the USA, it is more common to refer to such systems by the more specific term, "GPS", because in almost all cases US satellite navigation systems only make use of the Global Positioning System fleet of satellites.

SCI-FI

What an amazing genre of entertainment Science Fiction, or *sci-fi*, is! Books, movies, radio shows, comics and artwork have thrilled and inspired generations of people for hundreds of years. The author of this small tome is no exception, having enjoyed the exploits in countless 1950s black and white sci-fi movies as well as current cinematic masterpieces. I also used to await the weekly arrival of the mobile library van in our small Somerset village eagerly, at least until I had read every single sci-fi book in the collection. Of course, so much of the technology described in sci-fi books has now become reality rather than fiction.

The earliest known fictional work that included themes such as travel into outer space, alien life and wars between planets is the novel, *A True Story*, by Lucian of Samosata, written in the second century AD. Although the novel is written in the Ancient Greek language, Lucian was of Assyrian descent.

SEE-SAW

A staple of children's playgrounds, a *see-saw* is most commonly a long board supported by a pivot in the middle. One person sits at each end. As the person at one end rises up from the ground, the person at the other end descends. The people keep the alternating motion going by pushing up from the ground with their legs. This alternation is amply reflected in the reduplication of the name, see-saw.

The singing rhyme, "See-saw, Marjery Daw" was often sung by children riding a see-saw. The song appeared with its current lyrics in *Mother Goose's Melody*, published in London in 1765. The tune that is normally used as part of the song was documented in about 1870 by William Elliot in his book

National Nursery Rhymes and Nursery Songs. There is some indication that a variant of the song may have been chanted when labourers were sawing wood with a two person saw to help them keep rhythm. The phrase, "see saw sacke a downe" appears in this way in the 1640 Richard Brome play, *The Antipodes.*

Returning to the children's song, the most common lyrics are, "See Saw Margery Daw, Johnny shall have a new master; Johnny shall earn but a penny a day, Because he can't work any faster". Frequently the name Johnny is replaced with Jacky or another name. "Daw" derived from an early reference to a lazy person. In the Scots dialect, on the other hand, "Daw" meant an untidy woman, a slattern or slut. So an alternate, more adult version of the song "Margery Daw" was, "See-saw, Margery Daw, Sold her bed and lay on the straw; Sold her bed and lay upon hay, And pisky came and carried her away. For wasn't she a dirty slut, To sell her bed and lie in the dirt?" Charming!

SHIFTY-FIFTY

I have heard this term used from time to time to refer to a group of shady individuals numbering about fifty. Examples would be a sub-group within a larger organization, a management clique, or even an entire local government group suspected of minor corruption.

One slang usage is as a term for an unmarked police car. The "shifty" component means underhand, suspect, and the "50" is a recontraction of "five-O", a name for the Police Department as used in the television shows *Hawaii Five-O* and *Hawaii Five-0.* Hawaii is the USA's 50th State, so Five-O is a way of referring to the 50th State Police Department.

Euphemistically, a *shifty fifty* is a private repetitive motion of the fingers of the hand to induce a state of arousal. The implication is that around fifty such movements is sufficient to complete the task at hand.

SHILLY-SHALLY

To *shilly-shally* means to act in an indecisive or unproductive manner. It means to vacillate or to be irresolute, and the implication is that such behaviour is happening when the exact opposite behaviour is what current circumstances really necessitate. The term possibly derives from a variant of the pondering query, "Shall I, shall I not?" An alternate but less common meaning is to take one's time or dawdle. This may be a result of some degree of inheriting of the meaning of the similar term <u>dilly-dally</u>.

SHIM SHAM

Regarded by some as tap dance's national anthem, *shim sham* shimmy, or shim sham, or even simply sham, is a form of tap or line dance, originating in the 1930s in Harlem clubs and opera houses. At the end of many performances, as an encore, all of the performers (musicians, singers, and dancers) would assemble on stage for a final number called the Shim Sham Shimmy. Sometimes audience members would also take part.

I have a couple of times heard someone say, "Shim sham" when they really meant <u>*flim-flam*</u>. 'That salesman is a real shim sham artist", someone once told me. In my mind's eye, I immediately pictured the sales person wearing tap shoes, belting out a rhythm. Sadly, some sales people do indeed, at least metaphorically, tap-dance around <u>*nitty-gritty*</u> questions, being the <u>*flim-flam*</u> artists that some of them are.

SHINDIG

A *shindig* is a party or social gathering, usually an extravagant one, possibly involving dancing, often being held to celebrate an event or auspicious occasion. The term may derive from an earlier term with the same meaning, shinny, which in turn came from shindy, a game played in Ireland and elsewhere. Shindy, or shinny, is a version of field hockey played with curved sticks and a hard wooden ball, characterized by vigorous, combative encounters and teamwork. It is not too clear how shindig evolved from the name of such a game. Maybe the first party so named was a raucous affair.

To "kick up a shindy" is a term that means to cause a commotion or confrontational dispute. In Jerome K. Jerome's 1886 book, *Idle Thoughts of an Idle Fellow*, the writer says the following: "I always do sit with my hands in my pockets except when I am in the company of my sisters, my cousins, or my aunts; and they kick up such a shindy — I should say expostulate so eloquently upon the subject — that I have to give in and take them out — my hands I mean." For those of you thinking, "Hey hang on, shindig is not a reduplicated term!" I would simply ask you to not kick up a shindy.

SHIP-SHAPE

Something that is *ship-shape* is in sound condition, neat, tidy, well organized, and fit and ready for its intended purpose. Equipment can be shipshape; so can arrangements for an event. Management and technical processes and procedures may or not be ship-shape. The slightly dated longer expression, "All ship-shape and Bristol fashion" originates from the mid-nineteenth century when the port city of Bristol in Western England was at the height of its commercial sea-trading prosperity. The city's vessels had a reputation for being very well maintained and managed.

As an aside, the River Avon which flows through Bristol, at the point where it flows into the Severn Estuary, has one of the greatest tidal ranges in the world, sometimes approaching 50 feet (15 meters).

SHITTER-SHATTER

This is a term of my own invention as a child, which greatly amused my parents. While living in a very rural area of the county of Devon in Southwest England, I was in awe of the steamrollers that flattened and compacted the new asphalt (tarmac) being laid on the lane in front of our house. These were real STEAM rollers, powered by coal fires that roared beneath the water boilers. The hissing, belching and spitting steam that resulted powered two of these mighty beasts as they rattled, clanked and sparked their way backwards and forwards up and down the road for several days. Onomatopoeically, I christened the vehicles *shitter-shatters*. To this day, I still love seeing steam-powered traction engines and steam rollers at country steam rallies and fairs.

"SHM-" REDUPLICATION

The "*Shm-*" formulation originated in Yiddish, then transferred to American Jewish English, and has now become familiar to many English speakers in the USA and beyond. It is used in conversation to draw attention to something just mentioned by another person, generally used to indicate irony, derision, skepticism, or disinterest concerning the discussed object or concept. As an example, one person might say, "Shall we stop and have breakfast?" In response, another party to the discussion might say, "Breakfast shmeakfast! It's almost lunchtime!"

SILLY BILLY

A *Silly Billy* is a buffoon. Pretty much as soon as the Norman name, "Guillaume" became anglicized to "William", and the shortened epithet, "Bill" arose, then I fully expect that a Silly Billy or two exhibited their buffoonery. Certainly, King William IV of Great Britain was considered to be a right-royal Silly Billy. For more contemporary Britons, the comedian Mike Yarwood's imitation of the Rt. Honorable Dennis Healy, former Chancellor of the Exchequer, may be more familiar. Yarwood's "Mr. Healy" used the term *Silly Billy* <u>extremely</u> frequently.

SING SING

Sing Sing has been the name, or part of the name, of movies, books, songs, bands, a racehorse and other cultural items over the years. Sing Sing is probably more widely recognized, however, as being the name of an infamous American maximum security prison.

The Sing Sing Correctional Facility is located in the village of Ossining, New York, about 30 miles north of New York City. The land on which the prison sits was purchased from the Sintsink Native American tribe in 1685, and the name Sing Sing was derived from the name of the tribe.

SING-SONG

This is a fairly self-explanatory term for an informal, often alcohol-fueled and possibly impromptu vocal musical celebration. *Sing-song*s often take place in pubs. Where the pub is in a Cockney area of London, then at least in former times one might expect dancing to take place as well, transforming a mere sing-song into a full-blown knees-up!

SLAP-DASH

The only reduplication in this term is the letter A in both of the words, but it deserves a place in this book nevertheless, in my humble opinion. As a matter of fact, again in my humble opinion, the use of abbreviations that originated in text communication, but which have spread into emails and even scientific papers, is an example of slap-dash writing and perhaps of underlying *slap-dash* thinking. The abbreviation, "imho" to represent, "in my humble opinion", is an example of this creeping scourge. Furthermore, in my own humble

opinion, someone using the abbreviation "imho" is typically
not displaying or feeling humility in any shape or form.

Oh well, "slap-dash" itself as a term means unplanned,
careless, hurried, or of low quality. "The contractor did a real
slap-dash job pouring that concrete path. Lumps and dribbles
of concrete are scattered all over the lawn and flower beds."
An earlier use of the term was as an equivalent to slap-bang, as
in, "The waiter dropped the cake slap-bang in the middle of
the table".

SLIP-SLOP

This term is used to describe the motion or sound of water or
other fluids in a container, as the container moves or is
carried. It has also been used to refer to careless, awkward or
hesitant speech or writing (in a similar way to slap-dash).
Archaically, *slip slop* was a term used to describe sloppy or
weak food or drink.

SLIP! SLOP! SLAP!

In Australia, the beach culture and other outdoor activities,
coupled with abundant bright sunshine, has led to a high
incidence of skin cancer among the population. Numerous
public health campaigns have sought to educate people to the
risks, and to recommend preventative actions and behaviour.
The most prominent of these initiatives *"Slip! Slop! Slap!"* was
initiated by Cancer Council Victoria in 1981. The campaign
featured the character Sid Seagull singing and dancing while
encouraging people to *slip* on long-sleeved clothes, *slop* on
sunscreen and *slap* on a hat. This successful program was
funded by public donations. Subsequently, the initiative was
modified and extended to, "Slip, Slop, Slap, Seek, Slide", or
slip on a shirt, *slop* on 50+ protection sunscreen, *slap* on a
hat, *seek* shade or shelter, and *slide* on some sunglasses.

A similar campaign was used in New Zealand, "Slip, Slop, Slap and Wrap", where Wrap referred to wrapping on a pair of sunglasses. For the New Zealand campaign, the promotional character was a lobster named Tiger.

Other locations, including cities in Canada, have launched variations on the Slip-Slop-Slap campaign.

SLO-MO, SLOW-MO

These are common abbreviations for *slow mo*tion filming, a technique used extensively to allow fast action that would otherwise be impossible to perceive with the naked eye, to be viewed or analyzed.

Invention of the slow motion technique is credited to August Musger, an Austrian priest and physicist. In 1904 Musger patented a slow-motion filming method that made use of a drum with mirrors to support frame synchronization. The first public viewing of some of Musger's slow motion films took place in 1907 in the city of Graz in the state of Styria, southeast Austria.

SOOPERDOOPERLOOPER®

At the Hershey Park attraction in Pennsylvania, USA, the first looping roller coaster to be constructed on the East coast continues to thrill riders. Attaining a maximum speed of 45 mph during the 1 minute 45 second run, riders on the classic steel "*Sooperdooperlooper*®" experience the famous vertical loop, as well as a family-friendly course of small dips, drops, and bunny hills.

SPACE RACE

There is always a *Space Race* of one form or another going on. In the 1950s and 1960s, the United States and the Soviet Union were locked in alternating contests to launch the first artificial satellite, to send a human into space and then into orbit, to land probes on the Moon, to land humans on the Moon, to create a re-usable space shuttle, and to variously be the "first" to achieve selected space exploration milestones. National pride was at stake, but perhaps more importantly, the ability to demonstrate strategic dominance of the space around our planet was deemed enormously important by the military forces of both nations.

Since the end of the Cold War, many new players have entered the field of space exploration. Additional countries have sent astronauts into space and have sent probes to other planets. Private companies worldwide are also vying to provide satellite and space payload launch capabilities, to offer space tourism opportunities, and to enable humanity to become a multi-planetary species.

SPLISH-SPLASH

An onomatopoeic repetition of the already onomatopoeic word splash, *splish-splash* implies a potentially more continuous or perhaps aimless degree of splashing in water.

The 1958 comedy rock song, "Splish Splash" by Bobby Darrin opens with the lines, "Splish, splash, I was takin' a bath, Long about a Saturday night, yeah, A rub dub, just relaxin' in the tub, Thinkin' everythin' was alright". The song continues, with several reduplicative terms or pairings of words peppering the remaining lyrics.

A water park attraction in Long Island, New York called Splish Splash offers 20 water slides, rides and attractions, along with 2 wave pools, a large kiddie area, a lazy river, and other water-themed entertainment.

STINKIN' THINKIN'

Someone is engaging in *stinkin' thinkin'* if they are viewing circumstances or their own behaviour in a way that is detrimental to their own mental wellbeing. Alcoholics Anonymous characterizes such thinking as a factor that may drive someone back to drinking. Specific categories of stinkin' thinkin' include Personalization and Blame; Discounting the Positive, and Overgeneralization.

SUPER-DUPER

Anything that is *super-duper* is perceived as having outstanding qualities, or displaying excellence to an extreme degree. Many businesses and products include Super-Duper, of variations of the term, as part of their names. One example among many would be the Super Duper Burger restaurant chain, which serves the San Francisco Bay area.

SUPER TROOPER

A trooper is a member of a troop. The troop could be a military troop, a police troop, or presumably a troop of monkeys or any other creature for which the collective noun is troop. A *super trooper* would, therefore, be an outstanding member or example within such a group. The 2001 comedy movie, *Super Troopers* describes the shenanigans of a group of 5 Vermont State Troopers. A sequel, *Super Troopers 2*, was released in 2018.

SUPER TROUPER

Not to be confused with troop, a troupe is a group of performers, consisting of musicians, actors or other entertainers, who travel between different venues to deliver their performances. So a *super trouper* would be either a very accomplished member of such a group, or one whose troupe travels very, very frequently and extensively. A super trouper might spend all of his or her time on the road, with no home base at all.

A commercial brand of swiveling theatrical spotlight goes by the name Super Trouper.

Songs with the name "Super Trouper" include the 1980 recording by ABBA, released as a single as well as on the album *Super Trooper*, and Deep Purple's "Super Trouper" from the 1973 album, *Who Do We Think We Are.*

SWAG BAG

Needless to say, a *swag bag* is a bag for swag. What exactly swag means does vary, but in general it refers to items or property stolen or obtained illicitly from a rightful owner. The archetypal image of a robber in cartoons and films was a man dressed in a striped shirt, wearing dark glasses or a Lone-Ranger style mask, and carrying a sack-like bag with the capitalized word SWAG written on it. Whether any real thief anywhere, ever, actually dressed in such a fashion is highly questionable. Such an outfit basically screams, "Arrest me!" to officers of the law.

In the USA, it is not uncommon to see a pair of sports shoes ("sneakers") tied together by the laces, which have been thrown aloft so that they catch on and dangle from phone or electrical wires. Many teenagers find the act of so disposing of old shoes to be rather entertaining. That said, many people will tell you that if you see sneakers hanging like that, it means that, "The people in the house next to the sneakers sell drugs!" Notwithstanding the stupidity of most petty criminals, it is unlikely that any real drug dealer would advertise their activities so blatantly, just as thieves probably never carried a bag labelled, "SWAG".

But why, "SWAG" anyway? The etymology is unclear, but the term swag as used to mean stolen goods dates back to the early

1800s in England. A slightly later term, swagman, was used in Australia to describe an itinerant laborer who moved from town to town and from farm to farm seeking temporary employment. Swagmen usually slept outdoors, and carried their belongings in a bedroll, or swag. Ironically, in the very well-known song, "Waltzing Matilda", the "Jolly Swag Man" upon stealing a sheep, stuffs it into his "tucker bag", not into a swag bag.

SWEETIE-PEETIE

Although frequently heard, there doesn't seem to be any consistent meaning or use for this term. I have certainly heard people add "peetie" as a suffix to "sweetie", when talking fondly to someone. Also, it can be used in a cajoling way: "Could you get me an ice cream when you come back from the kitchen please sweetie, *sweetie- peetie*, pleasey please?" I also heard it once at Halloween, when someone said, "Sweetie-peetie, trick or treatie" while trying to extract a candy treat from a potential donor.

TATER-TOT

The name, "Tater Tots®", is a registered trademark of Ore-Ida, part of the H. J. Heinz Company. Tater Tots are a food produced from grated, deep-fried potatoes ("taters"), forming a small cylindrical shape. They are typically purchased frozen, and then heated in the oven before serving as a side dish. The crispy outside of the tots are what make them so appealing to many.

Tater Tots were first offered for sale in 1956. The founders of Ore Ida, F. Nephi Grigg and Golden Grigg, developed a way to use the remnant scraps from cut potatoes. The production method for the tots involved chopping the pieces of potato into small strips, adding seasoning and flour, then squeezing the resulting mixture though a small round sieve with holes, and cutting off slices in the form of little cylinders.

As a staple (and comfort) food in the USA, sales are enormous. Over 3,700,000,000 Tater Tots are eaten annually. Other countries and regions of the world have equivalent products. In Australia, for example, "Potato Gems" are sold.

As a side issue to this discussion of a side dish, a few years ago our son Nathaniel (*Nater-Tater*) announced that if he ever has children of his own, they will, of course, be known as the Tater tots.

A rock band called the Tater Totz released a number of albums and songs in the 1980s and 1990s.

TEENY-TINY

This term is one I used this very day in a social media post. I was explaining how I had come across a clutch of baby pond turtles emerging from an underground nest. The first sign that they were there was a single *teeny-tiny* head poking out and looking at me warily. I carried all 6 turtles down to the edge of the pond, where they happily swam away. Teeny-tiny, then, means that something is not just tiny, but tiny in an extreme or possibly in a cute way.

TEENIE-WEENIE

Very frequently used to accentuate the smallness of something, the term *teenie-weenie* will be familiar to many as the words that immediately follow "*itsy-bitsy*" in the song about the yellow polka-dot bikini discussed previously.

TEENSIE-WEENSIE

Essentially this is a variant of the above term *teenie-weenie*, meaning something very small. In some ways, *teensie-weensie* is a conglomeration of *teeny-weenie* and *incy-wincy*.

TEETER-TOTTER

This is an alternate name for _see-saw_, commonly used in the
United States. Its name may derive from the Nordic
tittermatorter. Other names used in the United States to refer
to a _see-saw_ include ridey-horse and hickey-horse.
Sometimes each of the terms used here may also apply to a
swing that carries two riders facing one another.

THRUSTER CLUSTER

Spacecraft and satellites often need to be maneuvered in
attitude or orientation as they orbit celestial bodies or transit
between them. Such craft might make use of mounted, small
rocket nozzles that can fire, sometimes in combination, to re-
orient or rotate the craft through each axis of alignment. Most
commonly, three or three pairs of nozzles will be mounted
together on a base to form a _thruster cluster_ to fire in different
directions as needed. These small rocket engines would be
powered by a propellant fuel such as hydrazine. (Some
spacecraft might avoid the use of such thrusters by, instead,
using "reaction wheels" as a way of inducing rotation.)

TIC-TAC

As with many of the entries in this book, this term has many
meanings and there are multiple spelling and format variants
such as tic tac, tick tack, tick-tack and others.

Most people will know of the small boxes containing pellet-like
hard mints and other flavor candies. These candy tic tacs are
made by the Italian company Ferrero. They were first
produced in 1968, they are sold in over 100 countries. The
transparent boxes have a flip-up lid. In some countries the
different flavor tic tacs are dyed in different colors, but in
others the plastic boxes are colored, with the tic tacs all being
white, regardless of flavor.

Until the late 1990's it was a very common sight to see tic-tac (or tick-tack), a signaling language, being used on horse and greyhound racing tracks in the United Kingdom. Staff of different bookmakers would signal to their managers the latest betting odds being offered by rivals. Signals also alerted bookmakers when a very large bet was placed on a particular dog or horse, requiring an urgent adjustment of the odds. Examples of the signals and their meanings and names include: The "double carpet" - arms across the chest with hands flat, meaning odds of 33-1; and the "cockle" or the "net" – fists together, right thumb sticking up so as to represent the number 10, meaning odds of 10-1. As might be expected, the advent of mobile communications technology has rendered signaling using tic-tac unnecessary. The terms for the various odds though, such as double carpet and cockle, are still used when relaying odds information using voice or text.

Other examples of tic-tac in reduplication include *Tic Tac*, a 1997 Swedish thriller movie; Tic Tac, a hiplife musician from Ghana; *Tik Tak*, a Belgian television show for children and the pencil and paper game Tic-Tac-Toe ("Noughts and Crosses" in the United Kingdom).

TICK-TOCK

Primarily this is an onomatopoeic term to describe the sound made by a mechanical clock or watch, as the various wheels and cogs, and perhaps a pendulum, oscillate or swing. By extension, the term can highlight the expenditure of time, especially as it is running out ahead of an impending deadline or catastrophe. "We need to hurry or we will miss the last ferry to the mainland, *tick-tock!*"

Used in journalism, a tick-tock is a step by step description of an event, or of the timeline leading up to it.

The Tick-Tock Model is a method of microprocessor chip production introduced in 2007 by Intel.

In popular culture, numerous films, books, and songs have made use of the term Tick Tock or close variations, such as tik-tok, tic-toc and many others. TikTok is the name of a social media video-sharing platform.

TICKY-TACKY

If something is tacky, it means it feels sticky to the touch, but not wet. I clearly remember that all bicycle tube repair kits (that every child had to learn to use) included as part of the instructions, "Allow the rubber cement to become tacky before applying the patch". So, when I first heard the term tacky used in the USA to refer to something that was of low quality or questionable taste, I was intrigued. This USA use of tacky to describe a person's or object's characteristics or behaviour derives from the longer term *ticky-tacky*.

Ticky-tacky mainly means that something consists of low quality or cheap materials, and is used especially to refer to poor quality suburban tract housing. The song "Little Boxes" that became a hit for Pete Seeger in 1963 was written and composed by his friend Malvina Reynolds one year earlier. A political satire, the song mocks the development of suburban sprawl and the conformist attitudes of its residents. The opening lyrics go as follows:

Little boxes on the hillside, Little boxes made of ticky tacky, Little boxes on the hillside, Little boxes all the same. There's a green one and a pink one, And a blue one and a yellow one, And they're all made out of ticky tacky, And they all look just the same. And the people in the houses, All went to the university, Where they were put in boxes, And they came out all the same, And there's doctors and lawyers, And business executives, And they're all made out of ticky tacky, And they all look just the same.

TINKY-WINKY

Tinky-winky is one of the Teletubby characters from the BBC children's' television show, *Teletubbies*. Tinky-Winky is the purple one with the triangle antenna!

TINY-HINEY

This term is used as a way to describe the rear end of a person that exhibits the characteristic of being slim. "Hiney" is a fairly common contraction of, "behind" or possibly, "hind-quarters", to mean buttocks. The origin might also come from *hinder*, a Middle English and Old English term for the buttocks dating from as early as the thirteenth century. Hiney is sometimes spelled as "heinie".

TINY NINEY

This refers to a small, easily-carried, low-weight, 9mm handgun. Usually, the low weight is achieved through the use of polymer material for the frame, in place of the more traditional steel. The reduced weight tends to mean that the felt recoil from such a weapon is relatively high, leading to possibly reduced accuracy. Some shooting enthusiasts find this limitation unacceptable, and hence another near-reduplicated derogatory term, "Plastic Fantastics", is occasionally encountered as a description of these firearms.

TIP-FOR-TAP

An early equivalent, predecessor term to <u>*tit-for-tat*</u> (see later in this book).

TIP-TAP

The sound produced by the act of tapping or knocking lightly in an alternating, repeating way might be referred to as *tip-tapping*.

Contrary to popular belief, woodpeckers do not drum or dill most of the time. Drumming is typically performed to announce a woodpecker's presence, usually to stake out a territory or to attract a mate. When looking for insects and grubs beneath bark, and even when excavating a nest hole, woodpeckers tip-tap at trees and branches.

A high-end restaurant called the Tip Tap Room offers exciting cuisine to discerning diners in the Beacon Hill neighborhood of Boston, Massachusetts.

TIP-TOP

Anything that is *tip-top* is excellent, in great shape, or is an outstanding example of its category. Someone could be feeling tip-top, or not quite feeling particularly tip-top, depending on their state of health. Tip-top can also mean the pinnacle or apex of something, such as a tree, or can refer to the highest social class of a country.

Tip Top® Bakeries, founded in 1949, operates 13 bakeries in Australia and New Zealand, employing 3,500 people and manufacturing over one million baked products daily.

Many other businesses include the words tip-top as part of their name or product lines.

There are towns named Tiptop in Virginia and Kentucky, and a ghost town called Tip Top in Arizona.

TITTLE-TATTLE

This is a mocking term for gossip, or for the prelude to someone coming forward to "tell tales" about another individual. The term conjures up images of elementary school, or behaviour akin to that found in elementary school (but conducted by adults who should know better).

TIT-FOR-TAT

A *tit-for-tat* action or utterance is a response in kind to something done or said by someone else. This measured, equivalent, retaliatory response can be engaged in by and between individuals, groups, opposing military forces, or countries. The term is a development of the earlier *tip for tap*, whereby a tip, or light blow, is returned in response to a tap, also a light blow.

A number of movies and novels have featured *Tit for Tat* as their title, reflecting the nature of the plot or narrative they relate.

In game theory, tit for tat is a strategy whereby someone will cooperate with an opponent at first, and then copy what the opponent has just done. If the opponent has just been cooperative, the person will be cooperative as well, if the opponent has not been cooperative, then the person will not be cooperative either.

In Cockney rhyming slang, "Titfer" is a term for a hat, derived as an abbreviation of tit-for-tat, which of course rhymes with hat.

TRASH-HASH

(Please cross-refer to the entries for *Hash-Bash* and *Hash-Cash* for background on the concept of *hashing* as part of running/social clubs.)

As an additional acknowledgment of the importance of sound environmental stewardship, some *hashing* events might take the form of an organized collection of litter and trash along a designated urban and/or rural course. In part, this reflects the understanding that the days of marking trails with torn scraps of paper (holding "paper chases") are long gone, and that amends should be made for such behaviour in the past. Anyway, needless to say, a trash-collecting hashing event is typically called a *trash-hash*.

TRICKY-DICKY

This appellation was most famously bestowed upon Richard Milhous Nixon (January 9, 1913 – April 22, 1994) the 37th president of the United States, who served from 1969 to 1974.

During his second term, much of Nixon's political support evaporated as a result of the escalating Watergate Scandal. On August 9, 1974, Nixon became the first American president to resign from office. His resignation avoided almost certain impeachment and removal from office. He was subsequently pardoned, controversially, by his successor Gerald Ford. During almost 20 years of retirement, Nixon wrote his memoirs and many other books, and travelled extensively overseas. As a result, he was partially successful in rebuilding his image and persona into that of a leading expert on international affairs.

TUTTI-FRUTTI

A type of ice cream or other confection that contains slices of various chopped, candied fruits, *tutti-frutti* derives its name from the Italian, *tutti i frutti*, meaning "all fruits". In India, *tutti frutti* refers to brightly colored small cubes of candied papaya, added to bakery products. Tutti-frutti ice cream appeared as a menu item in a New England diner restaurant as early as 1860. The concept led to recipes for other food

items, such as tutti frutti sandwiches, being developed and
marketed in subsequent years.

Tutti Frutti has been the title, or part of the title, of various
movies, TV series episodes and songs. "Tutti Frutti", the 1955
song recorded by Little Richard, contains the opening line,
""A-wop-bop-a-loo-bop-a-wop-bam-boom!" In April 2012,
Rolling Stone magazine stated that this had to be the most
inspired rock lyric ever recorded.

TWIRLY-WHIRLY

There is a children's toy produced my Hohner called the
Twirly Whirly Action Rainmaker. It takes the form of a
transparent segmented plastic tube containing multi colored
plastic beads that tumble across discs and spirals that spin
when the tube is inverted. The toy is a development of the
rainstick, thought to have been invented by the Mapuches, an
indigenous group from south-central Chile and southwestern
Argentina. Rainsticks were made from hollow stems of cactus,
with the spines removed, dried, and then reinserted like nails
into the dried cactus tube. The tube was then filled with small
pebbles, which would make a sound like rain as they fell over
the spines inside the sealed tube.

The term twirly-whirly might also be encountered as a
descriptive term for anything that can exhibit spinning
characteristics. One example that comes to mind is a rotating
outdoor laundry dryer.

WAH-WAH

In music *wah-wah,* or just wa-wa, is a sound effect similar to
that achieved by moving a hand back and forth into the bell of
a trumpet. Other instruments can emit wah-wah sounds. A
wah-wah or wah pedal can be used with electric guitars to
produce this effect.

"Wah-wah!" is sometimes said to draw attention to the fact that another person is complaining or whining too much about something.

George Harrison released the song "Wah-Wah" as part of the triple-album, *All Things Must Pass* in 1970.

In Pennsylvania, USA, there is a town named Wawa. Headquartered there is the convenience store and gasoline station chain, Wawa, that operates extensively on the East Coast.

WEE-WEE

A term meaning pretty much the same, and used in pretty much the same way, as *pee-pee*.

WHACKY BACCY

This refers to any type of herbal substance of questionable legality that might be used instead of tobacco in cigarettes or pipes.

WHAM-BAM

It is hard to hear or say this term without mentally uttering the follow-on phrase, "Thank you ma'am!" Well, it is for me, anyway! *Wham-bam* in its stand-alone form is simply an onomatopoeic way of describing a sudden event. The usage that springs to mind for me, as alluded to above, is a way of describing a brief but enjoyable amorous encounter.

Separately from all of this, or at least I suspect so, a 1976 song by the American group "Silver" bore the title "Wham Bam". On the paper sleeve for the record, the title was shown as "Wham Bam Shang-A-Lang", reflecting the chorus of the song, "We've got a wham bam shang-a-lang and a sha-la-la-la-

la-la babe. Wham bam shang-a-lang and a sha-la-la-la-la-la babe". The record reached sixteenth position on the US "Billboard Hot 100" for the week of October 2, 1976. The song is part of the soundtrack for the 2017 Marvel Studios sequel film, *Guardians of the Galaxy Vol. 2*.

WHAMMER-HAMMER

A *whammer hammer* is a style of small hammer, principally used by jewelry crafters and hobbyists. An earlier Whillans Whammer was a form of ice axe/piton hammer combination, designed by mountaineer Don Whillans for use on the 1970 South Face Annapurna expedition.

WHAMMER-JAMMER

A song by The J. Geils Band, "Whammer Jammer" was released on the band's second studio album, *The Morning After*, in 1971.

WHICH WICH®

The casual restaurant chain, "Which Wich Superior Sandwiches" opened in 2003. It is headquartered in Dallas, Texas. The chain has retail locations across multiple US States and in many additional countries. A distinctive feature of the restaurants is the ordering process, involving the use of permanent marker pens to check menu selections on pre-printed sandwich bags.

WHICH WITCH

Used widely in popular culture, examples of "Which Witch" occurrences include: *Which Witch*, a musical written by Benedicte Adrian and Ingrid Bjornov; "Which Witch", a song by Florence and the Machine; "Which Witch?", a children's board game; *Which Witch?*, a children's novel by Eva

Ibbotson; and "Which Witch!", an episode of *Tom and Jerry Tales*. In the British television series, *The Worst Witch* there was an episode titled, "Which Witch is Which?" in Season 3.

WI-FI

This is term for a service or connection by which portable computing and communications devices are able to connect to wireless networks. *Wi-Fi* is based on the IEEE 802.11 group of standards. The name originated in late the 1990s and was intended as a pun on the term Hi-Fi. It was first proposed by the brand consulting company Interbrand, which had been engaged by a group that, in parallel, became the industry group called the Wi-Fi Alliance, which holds the trademark to the term Wi-Fi. As such, Wi-Fi was never a contraction of the words "wireless fidelity", despite what many might believe. The intention was to simply use "Wi" plus an arbitrary second word.

As a sideline, I remain convinced that when the Nintendo Co., Ltd introduced the "Wii"™ game console, the expectation was that English speakers would pronounce the name to rhyme with, "Why", to emphasize the limited number of cables necessary to use the console compared to other gaming systems. In practice, consumers decided to pronounce it as, "Wee". The latter pronunciation is now the standard. Nintendo states that the pronunciation rhymes with, "we" to emphasize the fact that the system is for everyone.

WIG-WAG

This term is most commonly used to describe flashing lights or waving signals that are designed to warn or alert people to a possible hazard, or to an item or condition requiring their attention. Some of the various examples I have come across include the blue flashing lights on the roof of a police car, a low brake pressure warning for truck drivers, a railroad crossing signal, a movie sound-stage "recording in progress" light, and taxiway holding lights on airfields.

Wigwag is also the name for a candy bar in Canada which is of the same formulation as the _Curly Wurly_ candy bar in England.

WIGWIG

Wigwig is a small hamlet near the village of Homer in the English county of Shropshire. Wigwig was an ancient township. Its name appears in the _Domesday Book_ as "Wigewic". The origin of the name probably comes from an Old English personal name Wyga, combined with wic, meaning "settlement". So the name Wigwig meant "Wyga's settlement".

Wigwig and the nearby Homer were the inspiration for the name (and the two main characters) of the 1969 children's book, _Wigwig and Homer_, by Philip Turner.

WILLY-NILLY

The meaning of the term _willy-nilly_ has gone through two main manifestations. When first used in the early 1600s, it meant that something was being done under compulsion, or without, or perhaps against, the will of the person involved. The derivation was probably a contraction of "will I nill I", "will ye nill ye", or "will he nill he". While the expression willy-nilly is still used with this meaning today, more commonly now the meaning relates to something being done in an unplanned, random, sporadic, disorganized, haphazard or hurried way.

WISHY-WASHY

Something is _wishy-washy_ if it lacks determination or is ineffectual. Leadership might be wishy-washy, for example.

Food and drink can also be wishy-washy: lacking strength, substance or flavor. Soup, wine and sauce have all been known to have been served up in a rather wishy-washy state. Of course, non-wishy-washy leadership by the head chef or the maître d'hôtel might have prevented the delivery of wishy-washy food to restaurant customers!

WING-DING

Most people will probably associate the term wing-ding with a series of True Type fonts called Windings®. When these fonts are selected within an electronic document, letters entered from a keyboard are rendered as "dingbats", visual symbols somewhat resembling traditional printer's embellishments that were often added around the edges of pages of books. The Wingdings trademark is owned by Microsoft.

The use Windings has largely been replaced by emojis, a series of pictograms, mainly smileys and ideograms, which first appeared on Japanese mobile phones in 1997. The name emoji came from "*e*" meaning picture, and *moji* meaning character. There is no connection between the words emoji and emoticon, but the latter was indeed a precursor to emojis. Emoticons are arrangements of typed symbols (mainly punctuation marks) to make approximations or faces, expressions or body parts. Examples include a colon ":" followed by a closed parenthesis ")" to represent a smiley face; the same, but with a semicolon, to indicate a winking smiley face ;); and (.)(.) to represent human breasts, and others.

Although most might assume that emoticons are recent in origin, there is a belief that the first recorded use was by the poet Robert Herrick in 1648, were he used the following in a poem: ":Tumble me down, and I will sit: Upon my ruins, (smiling yet:)". Another claimed early use was in a New York Times transcript of a speech by President Abraham Lincoln in 1862. Part of the transcript included, "... there is no precedent for your being here yourselves, (applause and laughter ;) and I offer, in justification of myself and you, that I have found nothing in the Constitution against." Both of these examples are hotly disputed, with many claiming that they were merely typographic errors.

OK, enough about typsetting! Let's get back to Wing Ding. One dated use of the term was as a description of a wild or raucous party or social gathering. To this end, I recall the term Wing Ding being used as the name of a party held to celebrate the return of an entire Air Force Wing (three squadrons) from a practice tactical deployment exercise. I dislike the beer Warsteiner to this day!

WOCKA WOCKA

With many variant spellings, *Wocka wocka* has been used in various ways.

The Muppet character Fozzie Bear employed Wocka Wocka as his catchphrase when delivering his as a stand-up comedy routines. The performer Shakira popularized a dance called the Waka Waka. Someone might say the words, "Whaka whaka wee" when imitating the sound of cheesy nightclub music.

The Boeing CH-47 Chinook helicopter is sometimes referred to affectionately as a Wokka, or Wokka-Wokka, based on the distinctive sound made by its two sets of rotors.

WOOLLY-PULLY

In the United Kingdom a wool sweater is often referred to as a "pullover". During WWII a heavy wool sweater was introduced for members of the British S.A.S. Commando Regiment and for the Royal Air Force Bomber Command. The sweaters had fabric-reinforced shoulders and elbows, and shoulder epaulet flaps to hold rank badges/slides. Almost immediately the term *woolly pully* started to be used for the sweaters, possibly to reflect the perceived casual nature of them as an item of uniform. Today many other armed forces around the world make use of variants of the woolly pully, including the US marines, US Army, US Navy, US Air Force and even the US fish and wild life services.

WOOLY BULLY

"Wooly Bully" is a song recorded in 1965 by the band Sam the Sham and the Pharaohs. The lyrics were written by Domingo "Sam" Samudio. The song was hugely popular, and remains so to this day. It reached the number 2 spot on the American Hot 100 chart in June 1965, and stayed in the Hot 100 for over four months.

"Wooly Bully" was a rework of the song "Hully Gully Now" by Big Bo & The Arrows/Little Smitty from 1962, and this in turn was a rework of Junior Parker's "Feelin' Good". Sam always claimed that the inspiration for the changed lyrics came from the name of his cat, Wooly Bully.

"Wooly Bully" had lyrics that were hard to understand, leading to some assertions that they reflected coded gang-speak. Some radio stations banned playing of the song altogether. In actuality, the lyrics are a conversation between "Mattie" and "Hattie". The topic of discussion is the "Wooly Bully", a strange creature that was seen by Mattie: "a thing she saw that had two big horns and a wooly jaw". Later in the song, there is a statement, "Let's not be L-7". This was a reference to, "Let's not be square", as a square can be formed by holding fingers to make an L shape on one hand, and on the other hand holding them to make the shape of the number seven. All of this gave additional rise to suspicions of gang culture influences in the song. The song has an overall Tex-Mex sound. Even the rhythm is counted out in Spanish and English as, *"Uno! Dos!* One, two, *tres, cuatro!"*

ZAP-STRAP

The most common use of this term is for a plastic cable-tie or zip-tie, used to secure or bundle loose electrical cables into a more organized, manageable group. This same item is more commonly called a tie-wrap in the United Kingdom. *Zap-strap* is also used by some to refer to any sort of securing or tie-down strap used to secure loads on the back of trucks.

Recently, I heard the term used as a name for a grounding/earthing cable used to complete electrical circuits within an automobile frame. The usage derives from the reduced likelihood of sparks to ground occurring if a primary circuit is properly grounded or earthed.

ZAP-TRAP

Similar to the second use of the term <u>*zap-strap*</u> described in the previous entry, a *zap-trap* is a low-resistance or low impedance circuit designed to prevent sparks to ground in spacecraft or aircraft instrument payloads.

ZIG-ZAG

A *zig-zag* is a meandering, alternative pattern of lines, or a path taken that is of similar alternating direction.

ZOOT-SUIT

A *zoot-suit* is a men's fashion item, an exaggerated version of a formal suit. It has pants / trousers with a high waist and wide legs, pegged at the ankles. The jacket /coat is long, and has wide lapels and broad, padded shoulders. The style became popular in African-American, Latino, Italian American, and Filipino American communities during the 1940s, particularly among youth who wanted to portray themselves as rebellious or anti-establishment.

The zoot suit first appeared in the comedy act "Pots, Pans &
Skillet" of Ernest "Skillet" Mayhand. Zoot suits were made
popular by jazz musicians and performers in the 1940s. Jazz
bandleader Cab Calloway often wore zoot suits on stage, and
wore one in the 1943 movie *Stormy Weather*.

Zoot suits were felt by some people to be unpatriotic, as they
used a huge amount of material during a time of wartime
shortages. In 1943, a series of anti-Mexican youth riots in Los
Angeles became known as the Zoot Suit Riots. The suits were
later outlawed for the duration of the Second World War,
partly due to the urging of Los Angeles City Council member
Norris J. Nelson.